The Wall Speaks

The Wall Speaks

Written by

Jerr

Illustrations by

Bruno Solís de Campos

Dedicated to every fatherless man

1

Preface

This book may be hard to read for some because it is the father's side of the story and most men have only heard the mother's side. It will defy the feminine and sour the emotions that exist in emotional men. The point of the book is to shatter the feminine frame of authority that exists in each man's mind, and that can be a messy affair. After a man reads this book, he might feel like I stabbed him in the gut and left him alone in the desert to die.

The greatest lessons in life come with a price. Through uneasy pain a man will find his way back to mental stability. Once a frame shatters, all that is left is a void of despair. The important thing for a man to do is not retreat into the feminine frame from fear but to stay in the void until rational meaning can be found. If the book is hard to accept for a man, it is because he fears his own surrender. He fears giving up the only thing he knows. He fears the story of masculinity that his mother sold him being revealed as false. Or he cannot equate a rational frame to the emotionally weak father that raised him. There will be cognitive dissonance as I shine a light on the hideous beast that many mothers filled their sons' minds with and reveal it as nothing more than human. This can cause anxiety and fear to arise within as the current frame of reality unsettles and breaks. Do not despair but gain hope in your new knowledge. By understanding masculinity, a new reality can be born. The rational reality that exists outside the emotional reality of womankind. Be strong and do not give up. Look down and realize that it was no dagger that I stuck in you but a roadmap to guide you out from the hopelessness of life.

Listen to my voice as I lead you from the desert of despair. Turn the page as if you are stepping one foot over the other towards the oasis of new beginnings. Read and reread the book. Practice, practice, practice and look for positive results with women. Do not hold tight to the body of humiliation that has traumatized you since youth, but rather look to new beginnings and be reborn into a new spirit of dignity. *Let the failed feminine frame of authority die within you.* The frame that has brought you nothing but emasculation and heartbreak. Leave that frame to women alone to exist in. And most important, lift your chin and be proud.

Introduction

I could have called this book "How to pick up masculine frame", "How to be a man", "How to be a human sandbag against feminine chaos" or for the immature boys "How to fuck as many women as possible: Society unraveller." All options, some better than others. But I decided on "The Wall Speaks" because masculinity to me growing up was as distant and unknowing as a blank wall. It was as if some men had walls and others didn't. The men with walls seemed like greedy beasts that women would trip and fall over in order to please. A part of me resented this framework as I felt that their posturing was simple minded and boorish. When I saw an unframed man, I saw a man who appeared free and looked as if he enjoyed life. An unframed man was free to laugh and have fun while the framed man sat unmoving as if he were being kept in a prison of his body and mind. What I disliked about the dynamic, was seeing how women and even other unframed men would reward these walled men with respect, as if the wall itself commanded respect. The only thought that kept replaying over and over was why women didn't reward the men who tried harder to project their personalities. Women seemed to me foolish as if they didn't know their own sexuality. Looking back, I see my own foolishness and ignorance of a woman's nature. Now I see the rationality behind the walled masks of framed men. There was a method to their madness. They behaved in a disciplined way that commanded respect.

Just like ancient pagans who bowed down before their unmoving statures, women had the same desire to revere the statued presence of a framed man. Looking back, walled men were like amused stones who enjoyed the bounty of their discipline while unframed men wasted their time in fruitless expression as if they were tap dancing for attention. My childish mind felt comfortable with the jokers who danced for validation and who often liked the same infantile things that I enjoyed. The stone-faced men seemed boring and adult. Their posturing seemed unenlightened and unexciting to my immature mind. After becoming a framed man, I can see that my ignorant thought was the exact opposite of the thought of women. The dancing monkey type guys were unexciting and selfish to them, while the walled men were interesting and giving.

To understand why women love walled men, a man must rationalize his own walled experience. Why do framed men remain emotionally distant and why do they posture so? To gain respect and sex. Those are the two elements that unframed men want as well. But unframed men lack the needed tools and discipline to get their innate desire. They fear change in their personality. They fear letting go of their expression and the emotion that comes from it. They fear a masculine frame the same as they fear solitary confinement. They fear letting go of the familiarity of their reality and the comfort of receiving validation of their being. They shrug the discipline required of masculinity because existing behind a wall takes work and effort. When a man can rationalize the reason to exist behind a wall is what gives him the needed motivation and support for his "confinement." When a man is unframed, he will endure a lifetime of abuse and humiliation only because he himself shrugs the wall of masculinity.

The modern world is being populated with more and more unframed men every day which has led to men being disrespected on a mass scale. We live in an age of fatherless boys who grow up without fathers passing down the tradition of frame. The tradition of masculine frame like a torch has fallen to the ground and is close to being extinguished altogether because the torchbearers are missing from action. All the forgotten generation knows is the feminine frame of authority that they were raised with. These men have been taught to vilify their own gender and to raise up women as purer and more moral. This is massive ignorance that only sets up a man for self-hatred and disappointment. Each man is becoming like a doormat that women wipe their feet upon. This epidemic of worldwide emasculation cuts at my masculine pride as men are being left behind and forgotten to undignified lives. To be a man should be a proud and dignified existence. That is the goal of this book, for a man to see the reason to bear frame and to see a reason for pride in his own masculinity. Now more than ever, a man needs to transcend the self-loathing over his manhood and enjoy the dignity that was bestowed upon him. We exist as a species because we fulfill roles as each gender, man and woman. This certainty of existence is what helps individuals escape from existential despair and psychological confusion.

BE PROUD OF

YOUR

MASCULINITY

Unwalled

American

My mother left my father when I was two
years old. We moved out and into a rundown
green house across town, somewhere in the
middle of America, on the edge of tornado alley
and the ice belt; the beating heart of my nation. It
was me, my four half siblings and my mom. The
reason we left was because my father was a drug
addict and had sexually threatened my siblings.
My mom told me he once threatened her life by
sticking a gun in her mouth while high on PCP.
All those things I found out much later in life.
While young, all I knew was that he was abusive
(in a vague way), had a temper, and that things
didn't work out between him and my mom. The
reason for leaving didn't take much second
thought, we had to leave and move on with our
lives. I can appreciate now looking back that they
were protecting me from knowing the dark side
of my father's nature.

From three to ten, I saw my father three
times. The first time I was six and he picked me
up in a white Fiat two-seater and we went on a
date with an attractive blonde schoolteacher who
had a daughter my own age. We rollerbladed on
a trail and ended up at the blonde's house after
dinner. The young girl and I watched cartoons
while the grownups spooned on the couch. Later,
I remember him dropping me off at my house
and us both seeing a mouse run off the front
steps of the porch and into the grass. I remember
feeling immense shame in my father seeing my

9

poor living condition. A child's mind can be a wild west show of guilt and shame.

That was the last time I saw the blonde and her daughter. The second time I saw my father came some years later when I was ten. He picked me up to go to the Barnum and Bailey's circus with another date and her daughter. The circus elephants looked malnourished and tired, and the clowns did as well. My father groaned about buying me a clown-face flashlight that I sheepishly asked for. The new woman had a badly pock marked face with mousy brown hair as if her body had been decimated by some soul-destroying drug. She seemed friendly enough at the time, but looking back I realize she was just trying to figure out my father on how he was around his boy and therefore how he would be with her daughter.

The third time I saw my father was with the same woman and the only memory I had of that time was them leaving me in the car while they went off shopping in a grocery store. My father ended up buying the scarred woman's daughter a gift and forgot about me. That stung like a hornet in my heart at the time. I had just been a pawn for him to use to get pussy. Those are the only three memories I have of my father after my mom left him and I haven't seen him since.

After my mom left my dad when I was a toddler, I remember building a fascination with Batman. It went beyond a child's interest in comic book fantasy. My young mind saw a fellow orphan as I watched his parents gunned down in the alleyway. The gunman robbed him of his father just as the bullet of circumstance robbed me of mine. This trauma held deep within him and deflected onto something else, a bat. He built his persona from the fear deflection and used his abandonment anxiety for greater good. Bruce Wayne is the presentation of his childhood personality turn adult while his Batman persona is the masculine frame he was never given by his father. This role not a mere act for him but his true self. I saw this orphan transcend his childhood to help his society. His greatest foe the Joker symbolic of the opposite end of the spectrum of fatherlessness. The embodiment of anarchy and disbelief. His over expression a symptom of his unframed mental state. These two rivals both having the fear of chaos within, but only one pursuing the path of higher order. Batman representing the order of frame while the Joker choosing the anarchy of being unframed. Both defined by trauma but only one choosing to make sense of it by creating order for his madness instead of surrendering to it. This could be why Batman is popular more so with boys and especially the fatherless. This chaos and order symbolism sunk deep in my young subconscious as I wrapped a towel around my neck and leapt from the crumbling wall outside my house. As chaos surrounded my environment, I fell into fantasy with action figures in hand. The less power I had in my young life the tighter my grip had been on the toys that comforted me. Batman had all the answers and hadn't let his childhood destroy him. I would rise above the chaos of my childhood and choose the path of order.

My mom remarried when I was seven to a man nearly two decades younger than her. When they were dating, he was a real nice guy by taking an interest in us kids. But after the wedding he realized he wasn't prepared for an older woman (more experienced) and her five children, so he switched from nice guy to tyrant within days after the wedding.

He was a property smasher. When he felt like my mom or siblings were not respecting his leadership enough, he would become irritable and that irritation would climax into wrath, which he would take out on furniture and whatever property he deemed worth destroying. It was a psychological threat on everyone in the house. We learned he preferred our terrified submission to our perceived "disrespect."

Tyranny is a bullheaded short-term solution that springs from weakness. It works, to a degree, for control purposes but ends up poisoning the hearts of those living under it. A tyrant creates massive anxiety in those that exist under that frame of authority while inspiring their resentment and bitterness.

When I was seven, I can still remember hiding under tables and watching as my stepfather went on his violent rampages. My mind collapsed in fear and my personality was stultified. That fear of violence seized my body and mind into a petrified existence. I became frozen like ice within myself. The only way I could survive was to be a phony and to be agreeable to what I disagreed with. My heart became cowardly from the sheer terror of my home life. Avoiding wrath from my stepfather was a daily victory. And looking back, was ultimately a daily death of my growing spirit.

I speak of this because it had a major influence on my "nice guy" mindset and created a coward's heart which caused me to absorb a thousand humiliations into my adulthood.

My mother coddled me from a young age, most likely from pity of my circumstance which is hard to blame her for (women coddle from a sincere place, but they do not realize the damage this does to a boy's confidence in his belief of his own reality). This further decimated my self-belief as I became dependent on those that kept me in submission for their own psychological benefit; my mother for wanting to feel needed and my stepfather for wanting to feel dominant.

When a young boy is raised in a feminine dominant environment, he will be ingrained with self-loathing about his gender which will lead him to dehumanize his manhood. This will make him view being a woman as more humane than his own gender. Every man should humanize his own manhood more than he humanizes a woman; to view other men as he views himself. When a man thinks other men are "dogs," then he will also see himself as a "dog." That is why when a boy is raised outside his father's presence, he will build a self-hatred within himself that will take him years to overcome. It is when a man begins to have masculine pride that he will be able to achieve self-love.

Although my mother coddled me, she didn't give me any guidance or help in being a boy. She would baby me and then leave me to my own rudderless devices. I would hide in my room and escape into books which greatly comforted me. This allowed me to stabilize my thoughts by diving into the thoughts of others. My mother gave me a Christian religious instruction and took me to service multiple times a week which I am still grateful for to this day for its discipline and structure. My stepfather was completely hands-off in parenting and didn't bother to explain masculinity to me. Stepfathers and weak fathers will keep masculinity a secret like Wizard of Ozs who control others with the smoke and mirrors of their own masculine frame. My stepfather was a tyrant in spirit who wanted to further secure my agreeableness and harmless nature by withholding the rationale for his frame. In a way, stepfathers raise stepsons like daughters. This tactic keeps the keys of the kingdom in the stepfather's hand without fear of losing control to another man's spawn. Weak biological fathers will do the same thing from fear of losing their authority. They would rather keep the wall up while their sons suffer in identity crisis than risk losing power.

The ones in a man's life that profess to love him are most times the ones most dependent upon him remaining weak. My childhood was an example of this as both my parents benefited (whether they were aware or not) from keeping me in a smaller state than them. My attitude at the time was based on survival to the next day. Become hidden, become small and agree, agree, agree. This even affected my posture as my stepfather was a short man and as I grew, I became taller than him. From lack of esteem and confidence, I would slump my posture as low as possible in order to not appear too dominant in comparison. My heart and mind were stifled under this fear mindset as I believed more in the tyranny above me than the self-belief within me.

I do not want my reader to think that I do not have love for either my mother or stepfather. They are both broken spirits just like everyone else on the planet. I love them both in my heart and wish them well. We are all desperate and needy people in search of solutions to our own problems. And we may rob others of their dignity in a sloppy effort to preserve our own.

This is human nature.

The environment I grew up in made me clueless to masculinity and masculine frame. Being abandoned and neglected sets a young boy back in his spirt and creates a human receptacle for humiliation later in life.

When I was eighteen, I married the first person that I kissed. We both met in church and got married in a hurry to have sex. In my twenties I was villainous which came from being unframed. I was passive aggressive, moody and would hold constant grudges against her. This feminine and unframed spirt led to countless cruelties. The one masculine quality that I had was I liked to be dominant sexually and knew exactly what I liked. But because I was a train wreck of psychological baggage, I overstepped myself on a few occasions with aggressive sex. Many fatherless men overstep themselves a few times in their sexual explorations. It hurts the spirt but if the man is willing to correct himself then he shouldn't remain overly guilty. On top of all that, I had severe neurotic behaviors which made me unframed on steroids. (I'll write a book on overcoming neuroticism in the future.)

In my early thirties she cheated on me with a guy at her work. I never would have thought that a woman could cheat on a man. My mother and sisters had always projected morality to me. My wife seemed like an angel to me at the time since I was used to only viewing myself as the villainous one. When she told me that she cheated on me, it was not only my wife who had cheated on me but the one woman that I knew.

It was the greatest betrayal I had ever experienced and felt like a thousand needles upon every surface of my body for months. At the time I felt like I was unmoored from my own reality and was floating in an upside-down world of pain. It was a dark void of utter aloneness. All around me was chaos and uncertainty. My world had become chaos and I sunk into hopelessness from my extreme sex anxiety which had grown from my newfound disbelief in fidelity. Every shadow seemed darker and every smile seemed wicked. I locked myself up in a stupor and forgot myself to art which was my only comfort at the time. I soaked my pillow every night with my tears and sobbed like a baby. From that void after much time, the feeling of death became normalized. I was both dead and alive like a blinking corpse. The emotions had been drained from me and allowed me to see the world with a body and mind without feeling. During this time, I wandered for help on the internet and looked for men who had also been betrayed. Being hurt drives the spirit in a need for understanding. Why would a woman cheat on a man? What is the motivation in a woman's treachery? These were all the questions that I needed answers to which led me in my quest for understanding sexual dynamics.

I read other men's essays and forum posts to understand the reasons behind women's sexuality and loyalty. Locked in my office, I painted and became lost in my own subconscious. As I splashed paint on canvas, my thoughts obsessed on why some men bore frame and why others shrugged frame. Every thought I had was related to my own failure as a man and how I could change myself to be a man with dignity. From morning to night for two years straight I only thought of masculine frame. From this broken and lost state, I internalized the very idea of masculinity into my own philosophy which this book will expand upon.

My goal in writing this book is to help every man believe in himself enough for his own dignity's sake. To escape from the doubt, he was given by his absent father and dominant mother. The world is growing thick with men who were abandoned and neglected like me. A world of weak men who lack self-belief, who shrug the burden of leadership from ignorance or fear. We need masculine pride as men, and we need to fight with all our willpower to preserve our own dignity.

The

walled

garden

When I was growing up with a Bible on my lap, I especially enjoyed the book of Genesis and the story of Adam and Eve. Here were the first human parents naked and perfect in the Garden of Eden who fell into the same pattern of relationship trouble that we see being repeated in our lives. This pattern can be seen throughout history with woman being symbolized as chaos, the instigator of disorder. In ancient Egypt, the god Kuk was dual in nature with a masculine side represented as a frog-man who was a Bringer-in-of-the-light while his feminine side was depicted as a snake-woman who was a Bringer-in-of-the-darkness. The Chinese Yin and Yang also depicted feminine as Chaos (Yin) compared to the masculine Order (Yang). These symbolisms were repeated and consistent throughout time and place. Our forebears knew human nature enough to see man as order and woman as his own unraveling. This understanding of a woman being the "undoing of man" is important for an understanding of what a feminized society will become.

A man builds and a woman deconstructs. In Genesis it was Eve who listened to the serpent that inflated her ego enough to destroy the perfect order of her life. And it was Adam who chose Eve above the dignity of himself and followed her into his own destruction and suffering.

Man's weakness is when he surrenders his authority to a woman. Opportunist women will exploit the weakness of their men and increase disorder for them both. It is a man's responsibility to our species to contain feminine chaos with his authority. The chaos breeder ideology of "happy wife, happy life" fools men into believing that their women will be benign rulers over them. "Make the woman happy and life will be happy." This reasoning has led men to fall into weak obedience to the wants and desires of their tyrannical women.

Picture a weak-willed man who treats his woman like a queen by giving her everything she desires. This man usually ends up suffering as the woman increases her demands more and more from her own dissatisfaction-of being-given-authority before finally "exiting Eden" by cheating on him. Women cannot help but listen to the snakes-of-their-egos that tell them to push the self-destruct button in order to have an adventure of their lifetimes. A woman resents boring paradisaic-order with its reliable stability. If there is not excitement in a woman's life, she will create it. This arrogance in abandoning stability and undoing order is a commonality of female nature that has been preserved by archeology across the world.

Feminists in modern times are the biggest pushers of a disorder ideology called postmodernism which allows a person to view the tower of history as a tower of lies. It opens the mind to endless interpretation of past events which nullifies all the meaning that we depend on for preventing present chaos. *When something is everything it becomes nothing.* This ideology has been used by feminists to view all historical meaning as oppressive. It allows them to equate history with patriarchal tyranny and lets them view the past through the lens of a victim complex. The destructive narrative of postmodernism frees humans of biological meaning and its orderly parameters by allowing people to view all things as "societal constructs," including their own gender. It dissolves established order and fuels mindless nihilism.

Feminists in our times are attempting to gaslight an entire generation with this philosophical poison in order to encourage people to believe that their sexuality-is-nothing-more-than-what-they-imagine-it-to-be. They view traditionalism as repressive to their modern feminine expression. They believe (in their arrogance) that people can be remade and be molded into whatever image they want. It is hubris to the extreme and chaos on steroids.

Beware of those that try to destroy history because what they are trying to destroy is the collective memory that protects those in the present. Postmodernism is a sledgehammer to the base of civilization. There are two George Orwell quotes that can protect us from this threat on our minds. The first quote helps us to be wise to their tactic, "Who controls the past, controls the future: Who controls the present, controls the past," and the second quote most sums up post modernism, "Power is in tearing human minds to pieces and putting them together again in new shapes of your own choosing."

Feminists are trying to destroy history in order to have complete control over the current generation of minds. These power mad feminists want to destroy all the history of female symbolism that reveals their true nature. They do not want young minds to know that the psychology of women is common to what our ancestors experienced and has been painted on cave walls for millennia. History is the enemy of feminists and so they wage war on history. To them, all history starts mid-twentieth century. These power-mad feminists wage war on religion because of its traditional family framework and established gender roles. All ancient symbols of feminine nature must be protected in order to protect ourselves and our ailing civilization from exploitation from feminine authority.

Feminists, on the backs of the gender fluid movement, demonize masculinity because masculinity is a threat to the sexuality-without-order celebration that they want to spread across the world. A feminized society is a beast that feeds on the weak corpse of masculinity. These genderless beings want all masculine frame to be vilified as "toxic." They will gaslight young men into viewing masculine frame as evil and retrograde to their feminine chaos vision. This feminist hatred and persecution will continue in its strength until masculinity has become outlawed.

A man is not born with masculine frame, he is given it by a caring father. With the rise of single mothers having complete psychological control over boys, we are seeing masculine frame fading from our societies. It is a tradition that we-the-fatherless and forgotten must pass to our fellow male orphans. It is critical in our times to not only pick-up frame for our own benefit but to pass it to the next man for his benefit. This is how we fight against the feminist hate that is surrounding us all.

A MAN WHO

LOWERS HIMSELF

TO HIS WOMAN HAS

HELL ABOVE

Women

lead

astray

Women want two sides of the same coin at once. They want a strong confident leader who has a vulnerable side. A woman's wants are just as unstable as her hormones and feelings. The following is basic information, but it needs to be reiterated to understand the bigger picture of a woman's psychology. Each month of a woman's menstrual cycle she will crave different elements, depending on which phase she is in. If she is in the Follicular phase (up cycle), she will crave aggressive dominance from her man while during the Luteal phase (down cycle) she will want more vulnerability from him. Every month, up and down. *A woman's mind is like a coin.* Her hormones flip the coin every two weeks to a new person, with new desires and wants. She is dual in nature because her body forces her to be. This duality creates a feeling of irrationality inside her. She is full of doubt because she is forced by her body into uncertainty. This causes confusion as she changes her mind from one thought to the next. That is why women represent chaos compared to the more stabilized emotions within the body of man. When men have emotional issues, it is more based on psychology or substance abuse and less on hormone flux. A woman has emotional issues by design. This chaos within her is like dueling spirts that pull her away from having certitude over her desires.

They clash with options that ring in her ears when she attempts to make a rational decision. Half the month a woman craves "bad boys" while the other half she craves "nice guys." When a woman is in her Follicular phase prior to ovulation, she will want to find the type of man who is most primed to impregnate her (protector) and when she is in her Luteal phase, she will attempt to find a man willing to provide for her pregnancy. A woman's monthly cycle set the frame for the desire she has in sexual selection.

A "bad boy" is a man more focused on his own pleasure while a "nice guy" is a man more focused on his woman's pleasure above his own. A woman wants a man to lead her through sex and that is why she looks for an independent minded "bad boy" for her own sexual pleasure during ovulation. But a woman does not have control over bad boys when it comes to relationships. That is why she does not want to encourage this mindset broadly in society. And so, she will encourage men to be supplicants to her will. That is why a woman will only give "nice guy" advice to men and not encourage men to be "bad" She wants more power over men, not less. She needs a man willing to sacrifice himself for her sexual selection decision.

"But Jerr," a voice calls out from outside the page, "Women tell me to be a nice guy and that the best way to a woman's heart is to listen to their wants and needs."

A woman wants a strong man who has his own mind. What better way to see if a man has his own mind, than to say, "do this" and he does it. Doesn't that prove that he is weak and open to exploitation by his own eager obedience?

When women tell men what they want in a relationship is a shit test to see if the man has a mind of his own and how easy he follows orders. That is why it is key to ignore a woman's advice because it shows her independent will and thought. What women want is a man who isn't easily controlled and who has a mind of his own.

"But Jerr," the voice calls out again, "I see dominant women with weak men all the time, why would they choose them if they don't want to be with them?"

Because for a woman to be outside a relationship is seen as low value to other women in their social circle. Being in a relationship brings honor and respect from other women and tells high value men that they are not whores. In a way, they stay with weak men to exploit them of resource while projecting the good girl image for a possible passing king. If the right man comes along, they will be ready to jump ship from the weak man to the strong man with little guilt. The "mindless follower" type guy is merely a steppingstone for better things.

Women know that a strong man must be tested like a newly forged sword. That is why they mislead men with bad advice. Because a strong man would cut through their bad advice and lead them the way he wants. That is how they know a man will make a good leader for them. He must have his own mind, and nothing says a man has his own mind more than disagreeing with feminine advice. That is why most of this book will offend women, because it steals power away from them in relationships with their exploited men. They don't want to give up their unframed resource until they find a strong man. So they will gaslight their "mindless follower" type guy into believing that wrong is right, up is down and down is up. The truest expression I've heard in my own journey of masculinity is "Would you ask a fish how to catch it or a fisherman?" That is why it is paramount to dismiss what women say. Listen to framed men and after applying masculine advice watch how a woman's behavior changes. That is the proof in the pudding.

The

wall

itself

A woman does not love a man she loves his wall. The wall is a reassurance to her of him being in emotional control and makes him a figure of stability and strength. To be framed is to exist behind the wall of masculine restraint and control. To be unframed is to be unrestrained in emotional control and expression. The wall represents stability to a woman's dual nature. *A woman loves not the man but the wall he provides for her*. And if a man is unwalled, how can a woman love him? Think about it like this. A man's wall stands tall and proud before a woman as she touches it with her hands. It's cold to her touch and foreign to her emotional reality. It is unlike anything feminine she can imagine. A voice speaks from behind the wall giving her greetings. She begins to talk to the wall and tells the wall all about herself. She feels a sense of connection because the wall is a great listener. The wall doesn't respond to every little thing she says like an unframed man would. It is as if the wall knows exactly who she really is. She steps back from fear of this unknown masculine presence. Who is the man who speaks to her in short sentences and listens without over reaction? She thinks and begins to imagine. She cannot see this man clearly revealed like an unframed man who spells out for her exactly who he is and why she should be attracted to him. With the man behind the wall, she can imagine an entire world of strength and power within her own mind. And just as she begins to lose herself in her own mind the wall stands up and walks away. This confuses her as unframed men tend to never stop talking and never leave. This creates in her a feeling of indignation. Who does this wall think he is? Does he think he is better than me? She wonders as the wall becomes more distant in her view. Where is he even going to? She wonders and wonders.

Later that night she cannot stop thinking about the wall and who might be behind the wall. This pleasures her when she uses her feminine intuition and imagination in creating a backstory for him.

A woman falls in love with not a man's reasoning but from her own reasoning which is based on her emotionally charged imagination. That is why women will speak of being aroused by a "man of mystery." It is the mystery of the wall they crave, not the man himself. For if the man stepped out from behind the wall of mystery like an unframed man, then the fairytale would crumble apart before her very eyes. Her fantasy would die an immediate death from his revelation of his true self. A woman does not fall in love with truth, she falls in love with her prewritten fantasy.

"But Jerr," a voice calls out from outside the page, "If love is but an illusion then isn't that a lie and therefore not true love?"

LOVE IS AN ILLUSION. Love is an enchantment that we cast upon ourselves. It is a spell that binds those under its own influence with self-hypnotism. And better for the illusion to be cast on the woman's side than the man's side. When someone, either man or woman, falls in love, what they are falling in love with is the image within their mind of what they desire and not the object in truth. Love is magic and frame allows a man to become a magician.

When a woman falls in love, she falls in love with herself. Women are the most arrogant beings on the planet. Everything they crave and desire exists within them. When a woman falls madly in love with a man what she is madly in love with is her version of the man. She will love that projection of her imagination more than she loves herself. Sound confusing? It is because women are eternally confused about themselves. That is why when a society becomes feminized gender identity becomes confused and ever-changing. A spirit of chaos pours out from a woman's soul. The feminized society grows uncertain in sexuality which snowballs into a tidal wave of identity crisis.

When men pick up masculine frame, they pick up the certainty it provides. When men abandon masculine frame, they pick up a woman's uncertainty of self.

The masculine wall projects certainty to a woman. That is because women are innately full of doubt and uncertainty. The wall represents the anti-feminine in its lack of expression and with its strong emotional control. Women trust what is anti-feminine (as long as the anti-feminine is interpreted by their own imagination.) They do not trust themselves and they especially do not trust unframed men. They trust their own intuition in the presence of a restrained masculine frame.

A man must give up his arrogant self-expression and exist as a blank canvas for his woman to paint upon. Without a blank canvas a woman's imagination becomes muted and suffocated. Unframed men paint on their own wall with expression and women lose interest. Why? Because a woman cares only for her own fantasy based on her feminine intuition. Without a blank canvas she will feel deprived of her own expression and therefore feel non-existent. A man should never rob a woman of her imagination and deprive her of using her intuition.

Unframed men hate to exist behind walls of illusion because it is stifling to their own feminine need for expression. They want to be unwalled because they want to be seen and heard. In their mind, if they exist behind a wall nobody will be able to validate their existence and they will feel alone. Sounds like a woman, right? That is because it is a feminine way of viewing reality. The unframed man does not want to exist behind a wall because laughing, crying and talking makes his spirit feel glad…. also, occasionally sad. Moods go up and down. That is the "beauty" of life to an unframed man. The only issue is he must trade his dignity for that life.

The higher a man goes up emotionally, the deeper his emotional valley will be. That is why unframed men tend to be moody and unstable. But that is the beauty of life, right? A man can choose to live in an unframed state, but he should remember it comes at an expense to his woman. Acting like a woman robs a woman of her own femininity.

Only one can be carefree without frame in a relationship. The sex is better if the woman is the unframed one. If the man is unframed and carefree, he increases the risk of being abandoned by his woman for a man willing to exist behind the wall of masculinity. She would be fleeing a selfish man unwilling to bear frame for her. Remember that, a man bears frame FOR THE WOMAN'S SAKE. To build a wall is an act of love to a woman. That is why women reward walled men. The wall is for the woman's contentment. Unframed men only care about themselves at heart, even though they make a show of caring for a woman's feelings. They want the woman to appreciate their uniqueness and originality. They would rather be in the spotlight of attention with its emotional validation.

Being unframed is arrogant and selfish in a world with women. If a man truly is heterosexual and wants to enjoy sex, then he should make friends with the wall.

How does a man go from fearing the wall to loving it?

Two ways. First, he must grow to love himself and that comes from building enough internal strength to be at ease within. Second, after a man puts up his wall, he will start to see his woman reward him sexually. If the wall did not attract sex then men would not exist behind walls. Sex sells and so we build walls. This will help a man continue his walled journey.

Women are social creatures that shrink when not getting emotional validation. A man must practice not needing others for validation. The more he practices solitude the easier it will get for him.

A man behind the wall exists mainly in his own head and so therefore he should like that space more than any place on earth. Men

31

who struggle with loneliness have weak frames of reality because they depend on others for validation to stabilize their own. Why would a man be so dependent on other men's validation that he would ache inside himself? Because he lacks self-belief and purpose. Elements essential to being comfortable behind the wall. How does a man achieve self-belief? He must remove self-hate from his life and cherish himself.

"But Jerr," a voice calls out from outside the page, "I hate myself and that cannot change."

OF COURSE IT CAN CHANGE. Do not attempt to just wish it away without action because that is foolish. Work from external-to-internal and prove to your body and mind that it believes. Take the first step to self-love and your mind will follow along. Instead of eating healthy because you love yourself, eat healthy in order to train your mind to love itself. Instead of exercising because you love yourself, exercise in order to signal to your mind and body that you are possible of self-love. The external to internal approach is one of the most powerful techniques on the body and mind. And do not just include positives but remove negatives. Remove as much self-harming behaviors from your life as you can. Self-harming behavior comes from a lack of will and projects self-loathing to the spirit because lack of control over self is lack of belief in self. Lacking willpower over a substance is a ritual of disbelief. By drinking (my specific poison) a man makes his mind and body sick with his addiction. The more he fails to quit the more his self-hate rises. Self-control is self-respect and self-respect is self-love. The more a man gets control over his self-harming behavior, the more his mind will reward him with self-belief. A man must love himself in order to properly carry frame. Give up the poison by viewing your body and mind as a gift. This will naturally increase a feeling of self-love because you are proving to your mind and body that you believe in it enough to care for it. To care for something is to believe in its worth. Before a man achieves self-belief, he must literally start caring for himself physically. This will help him exist behind the wall of masculinity without having a panic attack. To have a strong frame of reality is to exist behind the wall without appearing anxious or unhappy. The wall brings respect into a man's life. And a man should not fear what he must become. But first, he must become strong enough to exist alone.

The second part that makes existing behind a wall doable is reaping the reward. This comes in the form of a stable relationship with a woman with an increase of respect and sex from her. (Two of the most desirable needs for a man with a woman.) Existing behind the wall does not feel so bad once a woman starts throwing sex and respect over the top. Once a man feels normalized to the walled experience and sees his woman contented then everything becomes worth the effort.

If a man is not getting respect or sex, then he is in desperate need of the wall. Masculine frame is an age-old tradition that has been passed down from caring fathers from one generation to the next. With the rise of single mothers, we are losing the tradition. A mother cannot pass down a man's tradition and too many men are absent from their children. That is why it is essential for us orphans to help each other up from our neglect and help dust each other off from the indignities we suffered without frame.

This generation of forgotten men who were raised without any empowerment have been overlooked because a generation of women have been empowered over them. The feminists that want female empowerment are the same ones who benefit from a generation of weak unframed men. These forgotten men do not choose an unframed state from arrogance but from ignorance of their own sexuality. The reason I am writing this book is because after empowering myself all I think about is fellow men who are being exploited and disrespected across the world. This disrespect fills me with immense hurt because of the holy nature of our masculine pride. Masculine pride is not just individual pride but a shared brotherhood of pride. A framed man deserves respect because a *man must bear the responsibility of all things.* As men we are born to lead and from this role, we must command respect for our authority. The world suffers when young men are forgotten and abandoned. That is why we must join together and become stronger than every generation before.

How

to

build

a

wall

Throughout history wise men have prepared boys for leadership with extreme-stress-rituals. These extreme-stress rituals would prepare them for the needed emotional detachment required for survival and leadership. The more brutal the existence for the tribe, the more brutal the ritual needed to be in preparation. Whether it was the Amazonian Satere Mawe tribe that would have a boy stick his hand in a stinging ant glove for ten minutes or the Native American Mandan tribe that would pierce a boy throughout his body and hang him up by his piercings to eventually faint from either blood loss or from shock. These extreme-stress-events would kill the soft boy and create a hardened man. Most times boys were taken from the world-of-women with its comforts and thrown into the ritual to be traumatized-into-the-world-of-men. These wise men knew that for the greater health of the tribe, young men needed to learn that the body and mind survives high stress. The boys needed to conquer their fear of pain and transcend the perceived limits of their own bodies. From the void of pain, the emotional trauma would overwhelm them, and the motherly lies of comfort would die in the ritual. When the boy passed through the ritual he would be welcomed with open arms into the world of men. It would start a separation between the sexes from a boy's gender-fluid state to the man's gender-solid state. The difference was made known through the expectation of suffering. A man had to earn his masculinity through pain and bravery. It was not merely given to him because of his birth. He needed to earn it by extreme-stress-ritual.

This cataclysmic shock to the boy's emotional-system would kill his irrational-feelings, leaving the deadened state necessary for rational leadership. Killing the boy's emotions would allow him to deal with stress as a man would, with a hardened mind. When shit hits the fan in life, whether it is war or disaster, men are the ones sent into high stress situations and expected to work through the suffering of their own expendability. The same was true in the brutality of existence for these tribes in the past. Each tribe depended on the hardened strength of their men for their collective survival. *Without strong men the tribe would decay and collapse.* Preparing a boy for manhood was an essential part of the fabric of tribe survival.

Nowadays with boys being coddled, they are deprived of the hardened state necessary for stress management. They have never had their emotions completely pulverized from the pain of utter despair. These man-babies walk the earth ready to crumble from the nearest sign of emotional-trauma. They never learned to detach themselves emotionally from their own bodies and continue forth with a feminine frame of reality that depends on others for emotional comfort and support. This unframed state only prolongs their suffering while further weakening themselves and society.

The only extreme-stress-rituals we have in modern time for weak men is either war or getting their heart broken. Unframed men with broken hearts go searching like outcasts from ancient tribes. They wander in search for answers to the trauma-void that they are stuck in. Killing a heart is a messy affair and after it's dead, it leaves only a mystery. An unframed man's emotions mean much to him, as they were an essential part of his ego, but after the emotions die, the ego is missing which leaves the man in a hopeless and lost state.

That is why when a man gets cheated on, he will search out other men to help him understand the reasons on why-women-act-the-way-they-do. This heartbroken man desires answers to his trauma and suffering. And if he is smart, he will not rebuild the same emotional frame that was previously shattered, but rather shelve it altogether for a rational frame. Just as in the past when tribal boys passed through their trauma killing the boy-spirit so the man-spirit can be born. Every male needs a rebirth into masculinity. It is not something we are born with, we must be traumatized and guided out from the trauma. Otherwise, we will return to the same weakened state, but embittered by existence.

My hope is for my readers to be searching for answers for their own trauma. If you experienced pain, then hopefully frame will guide you out. What makes suffering most difficult is when it lacks meaning. By rationalizing suffering, we become strong enough to want to live through it. By understanding masculinity, we want to be men. By understanding women, we find reasons for not giving up on them. By understanding trauma, we can transcend it and not be psychologically crippled by it. Life brings stress and unforeseen problems. When a man picks up frame instead of surrendering to his trauma, he will begin his journey to success.

The

wall

shields

her

      What is masculine frame and what makes a man unframed? Masculine frame is emotional control and expression restraint. When a man is unframed, he lacks control over his emotions and is expressive like a woman. To pick up frame a man must view his emotions and his expressions as enemies of his masculinity. This is all viewed as a negative from a woman's standpoint. Why? Because it is ANTI-FEMININE. Of course, they would disagree with this mindset. To females, emotions and expressing them are like sweet, sweet honey. It is how their system operates. But why would a woman see her way as not only the best way for her but would expect men to imitate her way? Because women only understand their own narrow emotional view of reality. They view the world through an emotional lens that is based on feelings over rationality. It is the only view they have. A man would never arrogantly expect a woman to pick up masculine frame. A woman is a female and a man a male. Each is different and has their own strengths and weaknesses. To want men to be feminized is small minded and arrogant in the grand design of things. Men and women are biological compliments to each other (if they fulfil their individual roles.)

How does a man pick up masculine frame? First, he must make a leap of faith to a new beginning. He must be desperate either from being sex starved or from being sick of being disrespected. Once he gets fed up with his life, he will be willing to make some hard changes. Second, he should view his body as within his control, not his body controlling him. For example, a laugh. How much control does a man have over a laugh? If something is genuinely funny to a man, can he control his own laughter? Or does it spill out of him without control? This could be the start of bodily control for a man. One way he could challenge himself is by watching a comedy that he knows will get a laugh and attempt to watch the whole thing without breaking frame (laughing.) Or he could challenge himself to telling a funny joke to his friends where he can set up the joke without laughing at himself. These are exercises to control frame breaks. This logic can also be applied to crying if the man is given to being emotionally sad. He could watch a movie where he knows he gets emotional and attempt dryness of his eyes.

How do these small steps help with masculine frame? Because everything starts small and emotional control takes time to train. (It can be done.) The body is within a man's control, that is masculine frame. We control ourselves by leading our bodies and do not surrender to them like a woman. Women are victims of their own biology while men transcend their biology. A man views his body as separate from his rational mind and leads it like a chariot under the whips of his discipline.

When I first picked up frame, the hardest part for me was in not overtalking and not over laughing. I'm a manic type who likes to ponder, and I got into the bad habit of thinking aloud and wanting to express my awesome thoughts to my woman. Talking is feminine and the more a man talks the less confidence a woman will have in his speech. Words are like currency and the more words a man uses the less currency each word has. That was the most difficult frame break that I had to overcome. The first day I picked up frame was unbearable and depressing. I felt I had all these great words existing upon my tongue which saddened me because I couldn't share them. But with discipline and the willpower to succeed I became used to existing behind "the wall of silence" and each day felt less depressing than the last. Also, the quieter I became the more my woman's speech increased. She was falling into her feminine frame because I had stepped out of it. This is how masculinity and femininity work.

A man sets the tone, and a woman follows along. If a man is feminine, then his woman will become masculinized and if a man becomes masculine, his woman will become feminized. The man controls the relationship's sexual dynamic. Men have the power if they are willing to seize it.

The more time a man spends behind the wall of masculinity, the more he will notice men without walls acting carefree. They laugh, they talk, and cry like women. The unframed men have their own perception, they view framed men as boring and without personality. To these unframed men, a masculine man is a posturing and selfish bore. They would rather exist freely expressing themselves in the belief that if they make their emotions known people will appreciate them more. Unframed men think that by telling someone that they are interesting will make that someone believe they are interesting. These men are fools and women resent them for it. Why? Because women abhor existing behind "the wall," but they'll pick up frame because someone in the relationship must. Not everyone can be carefree in emotional weakness within a relationship and women innately know this. Someone must command respect and take care of business. And so, the woman with an unframed man will begrudgingly pick up the man's frame like a fallen shield dropped on the battlefield. She bears the shield while her man skips carefree amidst the falling arrows of reality.

Without a framed protector before her she will be exposed to the chaos of reality. This builds bitterness in her because a woman has enough difficulty managing her own emotional chaos without having to worry about a man's burden. She picks up the frolicking and carefree man's shield and tries her best to bear his load. Sound unfair? Biologically it is incredibly unfair and that is why a weak man is more to blame for a woman's resentment than the woman herself. Remember, a woman is biologically at war with herself and is not equipped for the wall of masculinity due to her innate emotionalism. That is why it is paramount that a man bears the burden of frame so a woman can be feminine behind the walls he surrounds her with. A man who picks up frame allows his woman to fall into her feminine. A woman cannot control her own femininity because she exists innately as a compliment to her man and will pick up whatever he lacks. If a man acts womanly the woman will act manly. She does not want to, but she will feel such fear and anxiety from being exposed to reality that she will have to pick up frame for her own emotional protection.

A woman will reward a framed man with sex because of the great relief that he provides her. With him holding up the protective wall she can "let her hair down." The man's wall bears the brunt of chaos of reality which allows-her-to-take-care-of-him as a helper while having enough emotional energy for their children. This is the innate framework of man and woman.

SHATTER THE FEMININE FRAME OF AUTHORITY IN YOUR MIND AND BE FREE

44

The

wall

is

her

world

When a man bears frame his woman will be centered around his life. She exists like a moon orbiting around his planet of self. The stronger his frame the more she stays in his orbit. An unframed man who changes himself in order to please his woman makes his world smaller which makes his gravity less. This causes his woman to break away from his gravitational pull and float to a stronger man's reality.

The dual nature of women is that they want to lower the gravity of a man's world but will abandon him once the world is changed. Once his world is changed to her vision, she no longer desires him. Why? Because a woman wants an independent entity to orbit. She attempts to change a man to prove that the man is weak-minded. A woman is an innate orbiter and when a man's world becomes small it is as if two moons circle each other towards collision. She wants a planet not a satellite. And she will try her hardest to chisel a man's planet down until it is smaller than her own reality.

A woman needs the strongest unmoving object possible to ease her floating anxiety.

"But Jerr," a voice calls out from off the page, "My life is nothing and my woman is too good for it. I try to please her as much as I can—"

Stop. A woman is nothing compared to a man. She is but a human compared to your godlike glory. I don't care if a man is homeless. He can make his cardboard box seem like a palace with the right attitude. A woman's reality bends around her man dependent on how strong his frame is. It is a man's frame that is the gravity that pulls her in. Rich men with weak frames lose women and poor men with strong frames keep women. It is not the external material possessions that summon belief but rather the frame itself. If a man believes his world is as big as Saturn, then his gravity will feel like it. *Women seek strong frames.* A man's frame is weak only increases a woman's innate existential anxiety like a young girl seeing her father cry. Worlds melt when frames break.

A man should make his pile of dirt seem like a pile of gold. If he believes, then his woman will share the same frame of thought. She depends on a man's self-belief and certainty of his own existence. This calms her into a gentle orbit around his world.

When a man's world falls apart from unemployment, this offset of his own gravity fall throws off his Luna out into another man's world. But it wasn't simply the material suffering that sent her flying as much as it was the man's reaction to his own suffering. A woman is a mojo feeder and when a man loses his mojo she starves. If a man lost his job and managed his suffering by summoning enough confidence to quell his woman's fear, it would stabilize her reality.

This is what leaders are expected to do. They calm hysterics. When a stock plummets, a CEO is expected to show a brave face to the stockholders or when a democracy is in a civil unrest it is up to the president to be a fearless leader for the country. This "show of face" is what is expected from someone in charge at the top. Sound hard? That is because it is. Being a leader requires stress management talent. Not only for the self but for others perceptional benefit. To ease their worry and doubts just as a father handles unforeseen crisis while his children sleep soft in their beds. He bears the burden alone and in secret. That is the key to good leadership. A man must bear the burden of all realities. It is this bearing of frame that builds the strong gravity that a woman needs for her innate emotional chaos. She needs the wall to ease her suffering and to heal her worriment. That is the responsibility of a framed man.

"But Jerr," a voice calls out from off the page, "How do we bear this reality?"

SELF BELIEF. If a man believes in his woman's reality more than his own then he fails them both. It doesn't matter if she is the queen of England, she still needs to bend a knee to her man. It is in her submission to her man's reality that a woman becomes reassured of her own. That is why when women become leaders in the world the world will suffer a cataclysm. Women are not designed to bear the stress of reality outside masculine frames and when enough women rule the world, it will decline and fall from their hands. Only choose a woman as leader if you want to see someone lose their shit when a crisis comes knocking on the door. Hysteria is an unframed disease that is spreading across our earth due to emotionalism and the dying tradition of masculine frame. We must bring back frame to help men to bear the burden of reality. *It takes every man to pick up, carry and pass frame.* The importance is beyond what a man can imagine. By passing frame we can undo the damage that was created when an unframed generation of men were created by the welfare state that subsidized single motherhood. The welfare state robbed fathers of the dignity of their provider role and allowed women to escape into the arms of government security. This reality is a soft illusion. It is the government that allows the beast of feminism to exist. Without the welfare state many women would be forced to endure in their relationships instead of government assisted escape. These arrogant politicians created the feminist swamp that a generation of fatherless boys grew up in. Do not hold onto frame like a selfish animal that only cares about the meager power of the moment while mankind is being groomed for future slavery. Pass frame to your fellow man.

The

wall

speaks

Once a man exists behind the wall of his expressive and emotional control, the next step will be for him to work on speaking with authority. For if a woman approaches a big beautiful wall and the voice squeaks out like an uncertain mouse then she will lose confidence. This comes through working on the control of speech, content of speech and quality of speech.

Think about the control of speech as in the rewording of Shakespeare, 'To speak or not to speak.' When to speak and when to hold back words. Having control over speech is a masculine trait. When a woman asks a man a question, his response time is his control of his speech. If he responds too quickly, then he thinks little of the control of the flow of his words. The quickness of reply is seen as anxious and weak to a woman. If a man slows down his response by seconds with a woman, this shows her that he exists on his own timetable and is in control of his own speech. Another way is in the occasional dismissal of a woman's speech. A woman does not just speak to have a back and forth with a man. Oftentimes she speaks only because she is thinking out loud. When a man responds to a woman who's thinking aloud shows that he takes her too seriously which drains her energy. If her brave leader is overly concerned with her silliness then he is falling into her frame which creates anxious feelings in her view of his leadership. If what she says does not make sense then do not respond. Have the power to ignore. A man should not over speak by using too many words. The more a man talks the less his words will be believed. Why? Because the world is full of talkers and women know talking is just that, *talk*. Using less words increases the value of each individual word. When the wall speaks it should get attention and respect. If a man respects the currency of his own speech then a woman will share that belief. This is how a man increases the authority of his speech by CONTROL.

Next, we will focus on a man's content of speech. To receive authority, a man's speech must reflect certainty of his authority. This means a man must use words that are certain and that do not inspire doubt. "Kind of," "probably" and "maybe" are words that seed doubt in a woman's mind. Most men do not realize how often they use these words. The good news is that a man can mold his speech to whatever he wants.

"But Jerr," a voice calls out from outside the page, "What if I'm genuinely uncertain about something?"

BE CERTAIN. Most things in life are like a fork-in-the-road and a man must pick a path. A woman is plagued by doubt and uncertainty in her mind and that is why she craves certainty in a man because a man must lead her from her innate uncertainty. *Work on certainty*. Become immediate in choosing an option from multiple options. A man can train himself in becoming quick to be certain. It takes practice like all things. Say you come to a fork in the road with your woman by your side, you make a quick decision, "Let's go right" you say, and the woman might say, as they often do, "The path on the left will get us back faster" (this would be a small shit test), then your reply would be, "We'll take the scenic route." Another way to solve that scenario would be to dismiss the woman and start walking the right trail. Either way would solve the leadership dilemma.

The key is to decide and own that decision. This will reassure the woman of your decision-making abilities and calm her own uncertainty in her mind. The thing to remember is immediacy is needed because inaction also projects uncertainty to her. Be quick to make up your mind. An indecisive leader creates anxiety in his woman and is failing in his masculinity. Be certain by controlling the CONTENT of your speech.

The next aspect of speech we will focus on is QUALITY. When I was hiding under tables during my childhood not only did my body want to hide but my voice hid in the back of my throat as well. This trauma put me into flight mode in some aspects of my being. A man's voice can get caught in that flight mode and he will try to talk as fast as possible because he is afraid that someone will cut him off. This behavior is like an animal eating fast because it is afraid that another animal will steal its food. This requires training to SLOW IT DOWN. Remember, fast speech is anxiety projection and spreads fear to women. Another aspect to correct is when men speak from the back of their throat. This creates a pinched quality to their words. A man must speak from his diaphragm which allows him a relaxed deep resonance. Work on breathing deeply from the diaphragm and then speak from those breaths. One way a man can break up the squeezed fear that wraps around his larynx is to do primal screams. This is when a man opens his voice path and shouts as loud as he can. This breaks apart the neurotic tension and held-patterns that were ingrained from childhood. This training in a sense is like talking the scared-child-voice out from its place of fear in the back of the throat. When the wall speaks to the woman it should be LOW AND SLOW. The wall does not speak high in tension and fear. And the wall does not need to hurry his speech.

The voice is not permanent in its setting as many believe, it can be molded. A man takes control of himself as if he were a machine in need of tuning. Tuning the voice down and altering each breath to be slower with non-rushed speech reassures the woman of the power of a man's authority. Work to improve the QUALITY of your words.

The

mystery

behind

the

wall

When I was a child, my mom would work to demystify me by inspiring confession. She would say, "what is the matter?" or "I know something is the matter, do you want to tell me something?" This trained me to exist in a guilt state with her as the frame of authority in my mind. A single mother is trying her best and that is why she uses shame tactics to control a boy because she fears him becoming a criminal. Do not blame her, for she is only a silly woman and didn't know any better. Later in life a man will naturally demystify himself to free himself of guilty feelings because he was trained to do so. This confessional state places a woman in a place of authority over a man as she becomes his designated redeemer.

To free himself of this pathetic state, a man must *shatter the frame of feminine authority in his mind.*

He does not need to confess to any woman, ever. What happens behind the wall stays behind the wall. This is a liberation of the spirit. No longer does a man need to feel guilt that requires a woman deeming him clean. A man confesses to God alone.

"But Jerr," a voice calls out from off the page, "What if a man cheated, shouldn't he confess to the woman since it was a betrayal to her?"

No. A man never needs to confess to any woman ever. He is free from his confessional state. The only authority above man is God. A woman's psychology in a relationship with a framed man is already filled with her pondering fidelity. That is part of the "man of mystery" that they so badly crave. To reveal harmlessness is for the mystery to be revealed thereby killing arousal. She exists in two realities like Schrodinger's cat. The man is simultaneously a cheater and faithful in her mind. This is the mystery that women both crave and fear. They want and do not want. Again, the dual nature of a woman. A man's wall preserves the secrets that fuel mystery and romance.

Single mothers love and hate walls in their romantic partners and so they will do their damndest to keep a boy from hiding behind a wall of masculinity. If a boy is free from the wall, then a mother can keep an ever-watching eye on all his behaviors. Many men are trained by dominant mothers to feel guilty in keeping secrets which robs them of the mystery that women crave in their leaders. *A man cannot have mystery unless he is willing to have secrets.* The reason that men cannot hold a secret comes from a lack of belief in their individual sovereignty. Their mothers inspired self-doubt deeply into their spirits. A man who cannot hide himself is still controlled by this mother complex. To these men I will repeat:

SHATTER THE FEMININE FRAME OF AUTHORITY IN YOUR MIND AND BE FREE.

Destroy the mother's authority and become free to rule yourself. To be a man is to be separated from a woman's authority. To have power over a woman, a man must reject her power over him. To have dignity, a man must have secrets. To reveal secrets is to become harmless like a child. And a woman punishes a man's harmlessness. Why? Because a woman needs a man to be freed from her authority for him to lead them both to victory. In the past when women became pregnant and didn't have the modern ease and comfort they have now, they would have to depend on a man with their lives. It was up to the man to protect and provide for the woman while she was carrying a child in her womb. This innate need for a protector makes a woman fear when the man acts like a child with her. If he cannot bear his own mental state (guilt) then how can he have the mind to bear the reality for them both?

A man needs to be secretive in order to reassure a woman of his mental strength. To be overwhelmed by guilt is a sign of weakness within a man's internal frame of reality. Handle your own load and do not pour it out on the poor woman. Another reason why men want to unload their secrets onto women is because they view their women as peers and friends. She is not your friend or peer; she is your woman (romantic partner.) She is dependent on you not being dependent on her. That requires you to have a separate mind and conscience that does not require her validation. To require her validation is to place her above you in authority. That signals to her that you are weak and cannot lead her. It is important for a man to maintain mystery for his own woman's peace of mind. That is one reason why a woman craves a "man of mystery" because he represents a man who is not beholden to a woman's validation for his existence. This mysterious walled figure reassures her of his authority while fueling her imagination.

Keep secrets from her and do not feel guilt for it. This is anti-feminine and innately craved by women. It is exactly what your single/dominant mother trained you not to be. It is the father's way.

The wall hides a man's true self and only he knows what that self is. The woman may pick up on some clues, but she will create the rest with her imagination based on her intuition. A man who cannot help but reveal every little thing about himself kills the mystery and robs a woman of the use her feminine intuition.

"But Jerr," a voice calls out from off the page, "By being open with my woman, don't we draw closer together?"

It draws her closer to the exit. A woman does not want a friend she wants a fearless leader. A woman who knows a man's guilt and insecurities creates anxiety in her about him and allows her to build interest in that quiet guy at work. Never forget, she does not love you, she loves your wall. Without a wall of mystery, a man is nothing to a woman. When a woman sees a masculine frame, she imagines what he hides. And if man is not willing to hide, then he is not willing to provoke his woman's arousal.

"But Jerr," the voice calls out from outside the page, "This is all the opposite of what women have told me that they want in a relationship."

Of course, a woman told you the opposite. A woman is power hungry and wants a man to reveal himself in order to exploit his known weaknesses.

"But Jerr," the voice interrupts, "My woman would never want to exploit me; she loves me, and I love her. We are best friends an—"

STOP. Your woman is not your friend and she is not your mother. She wants the best deal for herself in a relationship and you should want the best deal for yourself. As of the time of this writing, women initiate nearly three quarters of divorces in the United States. That is telling of a woman's greed in wanting a better deal. A woman does not unconditionally love a man and in fact she has more requirements for love than the average man. A woman wants many things and will be greedy in getting them. By holding secrets, a man tips the scales in his own direction by being greedy with his inner self. Women respect a framed man's greediness of self because they share it innately.

Hold information inside and do not feel obligated to reveal yourself to her. Women will pry and pry but a man needs to keep his wall strong from intrusions. Secrets are what a woman desires and a man who holds secrets will keep her interest perpetually aroused. Behind the wall is everything she desires, as long as she is kept from seeing it. Let her use what she prizes most in the whole world to figure you out, her imagination.

The

wall

remains

firm

A woman's being is full of doubt and anxiety. This makes her emotional state inconsistent. Her body, full of hormone flux, is on a rollercoaster through the day, week and month. That is why she craves an emotionally steady man to help her with her own internal chaos. When a woman sees a stable and firm masculine wall, she wants to sit under its shadow to make herself calmed. Unframed men have emotional control issues, and this creates a dueling chaos that women dread being around. An unframed man fights with a woman in emotional validation competition. He lets his emotions control him which creates a dueling emotional rollercoaster with the woman. Both up and down, up and down. This emotionally exhausts the woman as she must frame herself more than her man to manage them both. It is a responsible thing she is doing but she will resent it because a man should be bearing the responsibility of emotional control. Men do not have the monthly battle of hormone, and that is why women expect more control from us, not less.

How does a man become less emotional than his woman? He needs to be disciplined in control.

"But Jerr," a voice calls out from outside the page, "Every man cries now and again. Sometimes I have good reasons to. For example, I—"

Stop. A man never has a good reason to cry and he should especially never show a woman his tears. If he must cry, he should flee her vicinity and weep like a woman to himself. Crying is a reaction to lack of internal control of self. It is an act of surrender to emotion. Crying projects that a man is not certain of his own self and leadership. And if a man is not certain, then how can his woman have trust in him?

Crying is for children and women eternal.

"But Jerr," the voice again interrupts, "You must cry every now and again?"

Yes, I do. But I cry alone and become ashamed over my weakness when the tears flow out. Crying is a breakdown of masculinity. It is repaired with the back of a sleeve and a healthy dose of shame.

To control negative emotion, a man must control positive emotion. When a woman sees a man acting overly happy this signals a fear to her that the man is unstable. Why? Because for every up there is a down and women know this innately. If a man is giggling like a little girl then he will be crying like one soon enough. A man needs to control his ups in order to avoid his downs. How?

Do not laugh overly. If something is funny then give it one tenth the laugh you normally would. By controlling expression, the body becomes stronger and will be able to control future expressions easier. By controlling uplifting expression, a man builds strength to control down expression. *Deprive the laugh to spare the tear.* Swallow those expressions and increase internal fortitude. This creates a firm and steady wall. When an unframed man sees a framed man, what does he think? "That guy is a posturing bore unlike me. I'm genuine and not someone who puts on an act." Unframed men see the wall as an act. They are half correct. It is an act, just like lifting weights is an act, but it is not phony. The framed man exists behind a strong emotional wall not because he is phony but because he is wise to human nature. The unframed man is unwise in human nature which allows him to be more carefree in ignorance like a child.

To stabilize the wall a man must practice, practice, practice his external behaviors. *External to internal technique.* By holding in a word that wants to be said, a man becomes stronger. By holding in a laugh that wants to belt out, a man becomes stronger. By holding in a tear that wants to be shed, a man becomes stronger. After training for a while, a man has less and less difficulty in managing his emotions. These practices stabilize him.

"But Jerr," a voice calls out from outside the page, "Women say expression is healthy and that being yourself is good for a relationship."

Ask a woman for advice about how to be man and she'll tell you to be a woman. If a man has a problem, a woman will say "be more like me." That is how they approach everything. A masculine man would never do this. If a woman has a problem, a man would not say "be more like a man." Why? Because a framed man understands gender difference. A woman exists in an emotional state because she cannot help it and so she believes that it would be cruel to make a man bottle up his emotions. What is cruel is how women treat men who do not bottle up their emotions. They become cruel to men who lack emotional control. They disrespect them, they betray them and ultimately, abandon them. And that is if a man follows a woman's advice to the T. Bottling emotions is what men do to please women. Women reward their men with respect if the men take care of their walls. Remember, a woman doesn't love a man, she loves the wall he provides for her. She needs the wall of masculinity to calm her anxiety and stress. She needs the emotional stability of a framed man. She craves the emotional distance the wall provides. She will not say that, but she will reward it.

Should a man's wall be completely emotionless like hard stone? Better for him to be emotionless like stone than to be expressive like water. The optimal way for a man is to be an "amused stone."

This means a man displays the power of his behavioral control down to a science and can showcase one-tenth of an expression. A slight smirk does more for a man than a shit eating grin. Masculinity projects confidence only when it's balanced in control. Balance takes strength. Not falling to one side or the other. By being an amused stone, a man shows his supreme control over his wall of self. Amused control is what women crave. If a man acts like a robot then he projects over-control and therefore weakness. To have control over expression is to be playful in its use. If a man is selling a joke and he laughs before the audience laughs; he steals the audience's enjoyment. A talented stand-up comic allows the audience to revel in its own emotion with set ups before offering release with a punchline. Frame allows others their originality of expression. It is selfish to micromanage emotion like an unframed man who wants a tight control over others by guiding them like an over watchful mother. The same is true for a masculine man and a woman. He sets up a feeling and lets the woman get off on it. This excites her and keeps her coming back for more.

Practice emotional control with desensitization therapy. If a man laughs at his own jokes, then he should practice telling jokes until he can keep enough frame to sell it. If a man has issues with crying, then he should place himself in situations that get him crying and practice holding it in. A man must practice "swallowing his expressions" and emotions. This can be done by watching a sad movie and holding in the tear. This can be done by watching a favorite comedy and holding in a laugh.

Exposure therapy and HOLDING BACK expression is where the power lies. A man holds back his power and doesn't let it slip through his fingers. If a man cannot hold in his emotions, they will spill out uncontrolled like a woman or child. Women crave this masculine control. Stability shows power and a woman will reward power with respect and sex, the two things unframed men lack in their relationships. Women pour respect and sex over amused stones. Most men are unframed and therefore deserve little respect or sex. When a man shows a woman that he is emotionally stable, he is showing her that he is ANTI-FEMININE. Women are attracted to what is not innately them because opposites attract. A man's penis makes him a male, but his emotional control is what makes him a man. This is important to the sexual selection process of our species. When a society becomes feminized, sexuality becomes fluid and confused. The lie of "just be yourself" becomes over dominant as women punish men who follow their own advice. These unwalled men prove to womankind that they lack independent minds and therefore deserve punishment. When masculinity reawakens in a society, men begin putting walls up and women start falling-into-their-feminine frames. What is important for a man to understand is that a woman is merely a reflection of him and not the reverse. If a man is emotional, then his woman will be unemotional. If a man is overly happy, then his woman will be overly serious. *A woman is nothing more than a reflection of man.* She picks up whatever masculinity a man abandons. She will do this with as much hatred and resentment as her body can hold. A carefree man creates a careful woman. The sexes in our species are compliments to each other. Do not believe the feminist lies. A man leads and a woman will follow his lead. If a woman leads in a relationship, the relationship suffers with her own resentment and bitterness over having power over the man. When a man leads, it frees a woman of the innate cruelty in her heart. All feminine authority is tainted with tyranny. Otherwise, we would see dominant women giving respect and sex to their men. These feminists have dead bedrooms, and they want to kill every bedroom on the planet in their arrogance. The rise of feminism lowers birth rates in countries that allow it. It destroys sexual pleasure in women and creates an environment of sexual poverty. The feminist mission is to weaken the walls of masculinity for the power to switch sides. That is why they encourage men to abandon walls and to become unframed. If they are so sure of their feminist ideal then they would be showcasing their stable relationships where the man has dignity. It doesn't exist because they are confused themselves.

Dismiss a woman's advice of "just be yourself" and follow masculine advice by protecting what you show her. Overcome the self. She wants a man who controls himself and that requires a man to control the weakness of his expression.

The

wall

stands

tall

Perception is everything. When I was younger, I was the kid that got picked on by bullies. The reason I got picked on was because I projected weakness and didn't learn to stand up for myself. When a man is being targeted by abuse, normally it is because his appearance projects weakness. Bullies prey upon the easy targets just as predators seek out the injured from the herd. They see weakness in a man's defeated posture which opens him up to more testing from them. Men who bully validate themselves by making fools of others. They see a man lacking backbone and so they test. If the defeated looking man does not stand up for his own dignity, this proves he does in fact lack a backbone which fuels the cycle of abuse. He becomes a mouse in the cat's paw to be played with as the bully keeps the cycle of humiliation going. If a man stood tall and proud then he would attract less vultures looking for a corpse to feed on. A man must work on his projection of confidence for his own dignity's sake. Look in front of a mirror and make sure the backbone is straight, the shoulders back and the chin up. This display of confidence lets a woman know that a man has a strong wall that won't get graffitied.

She wants a proud wall because she doesn't want to get hassled along with the man. If a woman is with a man that gets picked on all the time, this will create an environment of fear and anxiety for her. A man's wall of self that stands tall shields the woman from potential harm. A man who is slumped over with bad posture and who lets others humiliate him is a man lacking belief of self. If he genuinely believed in himself, he would protect his own dignity. A common problem with unframed men is that they expect others to defend their dignity for them. They will get humiliated and scan their vicinity like a lost child in search of a missing parent. They depend on others to defend their honor because they lack self-belief. Sound appealing? Of course not. A woman wants a man who is willing to kick ass if his wall gets pissed on. A man who doesn't stand up for his own dignity projects a weak protector role to women. A man should stand up for himself without any help. Why? Because all men standalone eternal and must fight for their own dignity.

Look before the mirror and give yourself a proud look. Do you look harmless or strong? A man should never appear harmless. That doesn't mean he should try to look like a thug, but rather that he should look like he would be willing to stand up for himself. Sunken posture allows the floods of humiliation to pour into a man's life. The world is full of those that prey on weakness. Give the vultures of masculine humiliation a lion's roar of pride.

Posture, although external, will create confidence internal. It is the external to internal technique. If a man summons enough willpower to stand tall, then this will reassure his subconscious of his own belief. A man sticking his chest outward tells the world "Come at me and I'll bite," while a man with a sunken chest tells the world "Come at me and I'll surrender." Which message do you want to signal? Project self-belief with proud posture and others will respect you because you are leading the way in that same frame of thought.

The

wall

commands

respect

In the previous chapter we talked about a man standing up for his own dignity. In this chapter we will talk about respect within a relationship. All women disrespect masculine authority to some degree, and they will test the strength of a man's wall. If a man sees a woman testing the integrity of his wall, does that mean she doesn't believe in him? No, it is a simple check. A "shit test" is used to check a man's wall for issues. It is a rare woman indeed who does not shit test at all and most likely it is due to her being controlled by fear. It is normal for a woman to test. But it is up to the man to pass the integrity test. If a woman shit tests and the man becomes emotional, the integrity check fails. If the woman shit tests and the man becomes violent, the integrity check fails. It is through CHARISMA that a man guards his wall. This reassures the woman that the man is not a tyrant. Because tyranny is a projection of fear of loss of control.

Unframed men fail shit tests because either they do not recognize them, or they overreact to them. Take for example if a man is testing out a car he is purchasing. If the potential buyer opens the hood to the engine and the seller becomes emotional in the overstep of these bounds, wouldn't that signal to the buyer that the seller is afraid of being found dishonest? And if the potential buyer opens the hood to the engine and pisses on it while the seller does nothing, wouldn't that also signal a fear in the buyer that the seller has zero respect for his own car and doesn't believe in what he is selling?

To pass a shit test is to not underreact or overreact to it. A man should recognize and deal with it IMMEDIATLY with calm charisma. The calmness of the wall is what reassures the woman that the wall is indeed strong with integrity.

Unframed men will get disrespected and will think about the disrespect until it sours their insides. Instead of being immediate in dealing with disrespect, they stew on it with passive aggression. "What is the matter?" a woman will say as the man pouts from her disrespect. "Nothing" the unframed man will lie and continue in his impotent-passive-aggressive state. Maybe later he will attempt to take it out on her in small ways. Backstabbing and poisoning are both feminine ways of warfare. A man who plots in secret ways to payback a woman is reacting to his woman's frame and abandons his own. If a man says "nothing" and it is not true, he is lying and lowering the currency of his words. This builds resentment and bitterness in the woman. The man will end up taking it out on her in more twisted and feminine ways. It becomes a battle between the two who can disrespect the other the most. And those relationships always end with the man being most disrespected because the man has most pride at stake.

"But Jerr," a voice calls out from off the page, "What if I fail to notice a shit test and I cannot stop thinking about it after a couple days."

If the shit test was small, then a man should just-let-it-go. If the shit test was big, then he should approach the woman. Most times it is better for a man to just detach-from-the-humiliation and learn a lesson for a future time. There will always be a future humiliation lurking around the corner and if the man has truly learned his lesson, he will be immediate in protecting himself. The keyword is IMMEDIATE. Because the more a man sits on disrespect in his heart, the more he opens himself up to passive aggression. To be passive aggressive is to be feminine in nature. Passive aggression is the modus operandi of unframed men. It comes from either a lack of immediacy or a fear of speaking up. When a man has been groomed from a young age to submit to humiliation, he will be naturally slow in dealing with humiliation. This slowness breeds resentment. But what he should be resenting is not the woman for humiliating him but himself for not standing up by natural reflex to protect his dignity. Passive aggressive men need to work on their immediacy. Their passivity only stacks humiliation, and humiliation weakens a man's spirit. This fuels a reactionary frame within them. When a woman sees a man becoming passive aggressive over his emotions, this projects to her that the man is weak and has emotional control issues. A framed man stands up immediately if someone pisses on his wall. He doesn't watch like an impotent voyeur while his enemies desecrate his image. How pathetic, truly.

The best way for a man to deal with disrespect is the classic phrase "Excuse me?"

which throws the ball back to the woman to think about what she did, then the frame is set to correct her with a calm spirit. Protecting dignity should be an emotionless reflex. It should be automatic to a man's body and mind. It should be as natural as breathing. A man must set the frame for his own dignity and not expect the world to naturally respect him. Respect is given only when it is first earned. Women respect because men give them reason to. The walled experience of masculinity comes through discipline and control. That is why women reward masculine men with respect and sex. They know how challenging it is to be ANTI-FEMININE. The wall itself commands respect, but a man cannot depend on the wall alone otherwise he falls into passivity and passivity is weakness. A man with self-respect does not let his wall get pissed on.

This advice transcends a romantic relationship. The world only respects those that respect themselves. It can be thought about through the Broken Window theory. If a neighborhood is in a run-down state, this will attract criminal activity. Decay breeds decay. If a building has ten windows and nine are shattered, then this will illicit less guilt and fear in shattering the tenth. The same can be said of a man attracting disrespect. The more disrespect he absorbs, the more will be given him. An easy target becomes easier. When it rains shit tests, it pours shit tests. The wise thing to do is to command respect up front. That way the frame of respect will be set for a woman to obey without confusion. If she knows a man doesn't put up with disrespect from the get-go, then she will be more apt to not piss on his wall in the future.

Receiving respect is essential for masculinity. And since it is essential to the fabric of a man's being it should be fought like hell for. Do not just let a woman think she can treat you badly. If a woman disrespects her man, she is disrespecting her leader and the relationship itself. A woman disrespects a man and remains guilt free because in her mind a real man would stick up for himself. If a man doesn't stick up for himself, he must not be a real man and women feel little guilt in disrespecting other women. Women are correct in their lack of guilt. A passive-aggressive-impotent-in-rage-being is not masculine and therefore not a man. This being is a male who has yet to pick up frame. And it is not a woman's job to help a man in finding his masculinity. Why would it be? She has enough problems bubbling up in her with her daily emotional chaos. A woman doesn't need more problems in life, she needs a problem solver. *That is why men do not expect pity from women when they fail at masculinity.* When a man fails to stand up for his dignity, he is not deserving of respect. Women are wise to understand this. Inside a woman's head she will think that if a man puts up with disrespect then maybe there is something behind the wall that she doesn't know about that deserves the disrespect. Why else would a man put up with humiliation unless he himself felt he deserved it? And if he feels like he deserves it then he shouldn't be trusted. This is how women shrug responsibility for their abusive behavior towards men.

Stop the abuse towards your masculine authority. The more a man stands up for himself the more his woman will join him at his side. She depends on you to set the frame of masculine dignity. Modern women have been groomed from childhood to disrespect masculine authority and they require training until their submission becomes second nature. A man deserves respect because he is the biological leader. Unframed men shrug leadership from a false sense of equality. They believe that relationship success comes from a peer-to-peer relationship. They are mistaken and confused. A woman teaches a man the cruel lesson of feminine authority when she disrespects him to such a degree that he leaves, or when she abandons him. Women are horrible at leading men while preserving the men's inherent dignity. Once they achieve power, they become tyrants with little regard for masculine pride. A feminist society wants men to fetishize their own humiliation in order to normalize feminine leadership. They know men will be humiliated under them and so they encourage men to enjoy emasculation. These unframed men exist in sexual poverty with a wealth of humiliation upon their heads. This emasculated state is the norm in a relationship with a feminist. Feminists create dead bedrooms because women do not have the same high sexual drive that a man has. When a woman is dominant in a relationship the sex schedule will be based on her lack of libido. A woman innately craves to be dominated in sex but for her to be dominated in the bedroom she must be dominated everywhere else first. To turn on submission just for sex is an illusion and women will have to live through decades of bad romance to realize this. *Sex starts outside the bedroom.* It exists everywhere in the house and a woman's submission should be in every room, not just the bedroom. For a woman to be submissive, a man must earn respect for his own authority. A woman cannot be submissive and disrespectful at the same time. By commanding respect, a man puts a woman into a submissive frame. A woman by nature will fight for authority and the man must keep her in-check throughout the relationship. When a man starts to command respect with a woman, he will create strong attraction and sexual arousal with her. Why wouldn't a woman want to have sex with a proud man? If a man allows his wall to be pissed on in disrespect, then why in the hell would a woman feel an attraction to the wall?

It is paramount for a relationship's success that a man protects his masculine pride by expecting and commanding respect with his woman.

The

wall

is

love

No other word has as much meaning to those caught in its grasp and so open to interpretation that it instantly becomes meaningless when rationalized as the word *love*. Love can be anything and nothing. Women and unframed men obsess over love because they are ruled by emotionally fueled imagination. This allows them to daydream with warm feeling in that unlimited interpretation. A framed man is more concerned with respect than love in a relationship because a framed man is more concerned with dignity. And nothing makes someone forget dignity faster than falling in love. Many love-lost men will abandon their frames because they believe they have found "the one" who will be able to understand the real man behind the wall. These men are anxious to shed their wall with the right woman. If only this "true love" did exist in a world where a woman magically became unaroused by masculine frame and started being sexually aroused by a man's true self. Doesn't this sound like a man who is tired of masculinity? He has become womanly in his desire to shrug the frame of discipline. Masculinity to this kind of man is burdensome and so he holds out hope for a woman that will look past the need for a man's wall. These kinds of men are more in love with their own personalities than the women they fantasize about. They want a woman who will love them for who they really are. If only a woman would love them like their mothers loved them, warts and all. See? That is what they truly desire. They want to abandon frame and emotionally depend on a woman who treats them like mother to child. They're momma's boys and cannot escape the shadow that their mothers cast over them. To these men, throwing away the old personality was too hard and so they hid the old personality in themselves for a future time when "the right one" comes along. These men will be punished for their arrogance in defying nature. The women they fall in love with will see them abandon frame and punish them for shrugging the wall that shields them from reality. The wall is love. Let me repeat that.

THE WALL IS LOVE.

A man who shrugs the wall doesn't love his woman, he loves his personality and fears letting go of his emotional dependence. That is why he will find any way he can to abandon it. A man remains distant not because he cannot understand love or that he doesn't have feelings of affection. A man exists behind frame because he has a duty to fulfill, he understands that a woman depends on his masculine frame for her own wellbeing. When I see a man cry at his own wedding, I always feel sorry for the woman. Here she is on her special day and her man shows her entire social circle a massive frame break that reveals he is emotionally weak for her. He robs her of the opportunity for her to be emotional before her loved ones. She must carry the man's frame in a wedding dress. Remember the golden rule of relationships, a man who abandons frame makes a woman pick it up. A man becomes emotional in love because he found his "true love" is a man who desperately needs emotional support. Does that sound like a man that a woman can respect? As soon as the wedding is over, the frame of the relationship is set. He needs her and she resents him. This will happen over and over with an unframed man (or a framed man who is weary of frame) because he fantasizes that one woman on the planet will not love him for his wall. Let me be clear as day to my readers. When a woman falls head over heels in love with a man, it is because she fell head over heels in love with his wall. She needs his emotional strength to enter her own femininity. She will reward him with sex and respect because of the burden he bears for her. He allows her to feel her own feminine nature. When a man "falls in love" with a woman he robs her of femininity for his own selfish reasons of needing emotional dependency. A man should not need emotional support from his woman. If a man does need emotional support, my suggestion would be to get a dog. Don't expect a woman to be the strong one in the relationship, this is cruel and she knows it. That is why women feel little guilt in punishing a man who abandons frame. They know it comes from selfishness.

"But Jerr," a voice calls out from off the page, "Does a man feel love behind the wall?"

Yes, a man feels love behind the wall, but he controls that feeling just like he controls every other feeling.

"But Jerr," the voice calls out again with anxiety, "Shouldn't a man let a woman know his love?"

A man should let his woman know his love but in a measured way where the woman herself knows it is measured. There is a scene in Empire Strike Back (the original Star Wars trilogy are excellent movies but many men overly obsess over them in an infantile way) when Han Solo in response to Princess Leia confessing her love for him replies with "I know."

This "I know" is worth more than a thousand "I love yous." A framed man knows a little goes a long way. He understands that a small gesture from a wall is greater than a grand gesture outside a wall. The framed man increases all his expression with self-enforced rarity. It is the rarity that creates specialness, and it is the specialness that women remember. A woman should be more thinking whether her man loves her instead of her wondering when her man will shut up about loving her. When a man constantly professes love to a woman is a sign of emotional weakness and anxiety over fear-of-loss. And there is nothing more repulsive to a woman than being with a man who is afraid to lose her. She needs a man to be emotionally, spiritually and physically independent. It is a man's independence from his woman that makes her dependent on him.

A woman doesn't love a man for who he is, she loves him for what he provides. Framed men provide emotional and physical shelter to women's emotional and physical needs. Affection in a framed relationship should be mostly sexual with occasional non-sexual affection. Most unframed relationships are the reverse. The affection is mostly non-sexual with occasional sex. And the sex is the "make love" variety which further shows a man's emotional dependence on the woman.

If you were a woman in that kind of relationship you would be resentful and repulsed too. Do not be too harsh on women, be harsh on yourself. It is a man's burden to bear and it is a man's fault for shrugging that burden. A man buys flowers for a woman maybe once or twice a year and he rarely buys her jewelry. I don't care if he is a wealthy man. If he gives her too many gifts it only signals fear of loss and falsely inflates the woman's ego. A framed man knows this and that is why he finely-measures-out his signs of affection. Affection should be rare to signify specialness and not anxiety. When a man says "I love you" to a woman every day without her first prompting it is fearful behavior. Most the love talk should be from the woman to the man. A framed man holds back emotion so the woman can be in her feminine by pouring out her own emotions. Unframed men are ignorant of this and steal a woman's opportunities for emotion because they themselves become emotional first. Do not be cruel to your woman. Keep the wall up and let her be the unframed one in love.

The

wall

fucks

The number one rule of sexuality between a man and a woman is "Is the man framed or unframed?" It is the frame that sells a sexual act and not the act itself. A framed man can be a little devil and the woman will share his pleasure. The woman's sexual knowledge comes through the man, she fetishizes certain activities because of him. He is expected to lead the sexual way. If a man is afraid of his own sexuality, then he is afraid of introducing a woman to new sexuality. A man leads sex, and a man fucks his woman. Women want to be fucked in confidence. When an unframed man "makes love" to a woman is more of the imitate-women-to-attract-women mindset. Women will not say they want to be fucked but that is to be expected because women want to be perceived as virtuous.

A woman craves a bad boy because bad boys are not afraid to be selfish sexually. Think about that. Women will go out of their way to reward selfish bad boys with sex. These bad boys are not reading poetry, buying flowers or spending half an hour kissing. These bad boys want to fuck, and women want to be fucked by them. That is exactly what a woman wants but she will not admit it publicly or tell nice guys that.

Fucking doesn't mean to abuse a woman. It means confident, assertive and rough penetration. When a woman is on her up cycle, she will crave this sex more so. Women do not want an unframed man fucking them because it is a break from his character and not in a good way. Remember, sex starts outside the bedroom. When a man is giggling like a girl all day and then becomes sexually dominant will confuse and irritate a woman. That is why it is crucial for a man to pick up masculine frame before he fucks.

Frame first, fucking second.

Does a man stop fucking a woman on her down cycle? No, he keeps fucking but he might temper it a small bit. A framed man fucks all month long. If a man wants to make love, then a man wants to lose a woman. "Love making" projects weakness because it is sex without masculine confidence. It is deflated and limp. It pours validation on a woman until she becomes flooded with her own ego. "Love making" is emotionally weak and projects cowardice. When a man starts getting confidence in a relationship, he will pursue his sexual desire without abandon. Sometimes unframed men get confidence when they have checked out of a relationship and get the I-don't-give-a-fuck energy. This allows them to start having sex the way they want. This inspires respect and arousal in a woman. And during this IDGAF phase, men will notice their women becoming more submissive and content. It is not an accident. A woman rides on the waves of a man's confident pleasure. If a man is seeking his own pleasure, a woman can be free to focus on her own. She doesn't want some unframed guy making googly eyes at her while she tries to orgasm. She does not need any pressure of performance during this time. A man who "makes love" puts enormous stress on a woman during the act whereas a framed man who fucks puts zero performance stress on a woman which allows her to sexually surf on his wave.

The stronger the man's frame, the more a woman will crave to be dominated by it. If a woman doesn't want to be sexually dominated by a man is because she doesn't respect him. A woman allows herself to be fucked by a frame she respects. That is the key to the pussy kingdom. The frame allows her to be in a submissive state for fucking. And being sexually dominated by a powerful frame is what most women's erotica contains. A woman gets dominated by a beast-like character who only cares for his own pleasure. If a woman is reading this, then she probably just got turned on by that last sentence.

Fucking is *certainty* and women like a man who is *certain* in his desire and *assertive* enough to get it. When an unframed man "makes love" he projects uncertainty over his pleasure and becomes dependent on a woman in leading them both through the sex act. Fucking is how framed men have had sex since the dawn of time. "Love making" is a fad in a feminine dominated society. Modern weak men make pathetic "love" to feminists who secretly buzz their clits to domination erotica. Sound like a utopian paradise?

Another reason why a man should fuck his woman is that it lowers her anxiety about his leadership. If her leader is having confident sex, then her leader must be confident. And if her leader is confident, then he must be at peace with himself. And this inner peace must mean that they are free from danger. That is one reason why a man should keep fucking even during times of stress. If he shows his woman that he has lost his mojo, then she will feel lost too. And when women feel lost, they stray.

Dominant sex from a man is submission training for a woman. Every sex act should be man as dominant and woman as submissive. When a man allows himself to be dominated sexually by a woman weakens her arousal and trust in his leadership.

"But Jerr," a voice calls out from off the page, "When I ask my woman to do something I like that is dirty, she tells me no"

A woman doesn't want to be held responsible for the dirtiness. There is nothing more of a sexual turn off for a woman than responsibility and accountability. She wants carefree fun without taking credit. She wants all the credit and/or blame to be placed on the man. Women will enjoy sexual experiences they would never have verbally agreed to. If a man introduces a dirty sex act and a woman doesn't tell him "no", then the man can assume silent consent. If a man takes a strong silent lead during sex, this will ease his woman into a fun-submissive-mode. If a guy is reading this and never had sex before and wants to jump into the deep end of the pool with a woman on his first go out, he will have issues. Usually, a woman will be comfortable with exploration of sexuality the further into a relationship she is with a man. When an unframed man asks a woman to do something dirty that he desires and if she verbally agrees, she verbally-shares-responsibility. *Unframed men love sharing responsibility with women.* This shared responsibility kills a woman's sex drive and allows her to easily dismiss sex acts that are not deemed "ladylike" She may want to do something dirty but openly saying it would kill the experience for her. That is

why a man should just go for it and be prepared
to stop if a woman insists on not liking it. A man
takes the lead in a woman's sexual pleasure and
if a woman wants to reject him, she is free to do
so. But most times if a man is assertively
confident then a woman will prefer submission
over rejection. If a woman says "no" better to be
safe than sorry. Being playful with consent is
better reserved for a trusted relationship with a
safe word prepared.

Sex is like stand-up comedy. It is about
timing, set up and execution. "Timing" as in
being aware of a woman's cycle and "set up" as in
allowing a woman to be warmed up to a dirty
idea in subtle ways. "Execution" as in not
projecting guilt or anxiety onto a woman about
your own sexuality.

When a woman gets on her knees, she
gets closer to her heavenly bliss. Facefucking a
woman on her knees is an ancient dominance
ritual. She exists for her man's pleasure and
allows him to use her the way he wants. Blowjobs
and facefucking should be standard to sex in a
relationship as it encourages a woman's
submission. When a man goes down on a
woman and licks her pussy, he puts himself into
a submissive position and inflates his woman's
ego. Imagine a man getting down on all fours and
sticking his tongue in a can of tuna. Lick pussy at
risk of losing attraction.

"But Jerr," a voice calls out from outside
the page, "What if a man enjoys licking pussy?"

If a man liked getting pegged, I would still
recommend he not do it for his own dignity's
sake. But licking pussy could be considered a
dominance act if the woman is tied up and

couldn't move. Then maybe I would consider it as okay and not fuel for her ego.

What many men need to understand about women is that their sexual imagination is incredibly limited compared to a man's imagination. The reason why is because men think about sex more and they must imagine their sexual plans before acting them out. This innately fuels a mind of fantasy within man. A woman who knows a lot about sex didn't think it up all by herself, a man introduced her. And that is what a woman expects of a man. She wants to be introduced to new pleasure. Many women are unfulfilled and bored because their men lack erotic imagination. If a man just thinks sex is sticking it in then a woman will become bored. And when women become bored, they stray.

Sex is not just about sticking it in, it is about getting a woman to get off on her own submission and anticipation of received pleasure. More dopamine is released in the brain during the anticipation phase of receiving reward. That dopamine hit mixed with the pleasure a woman gets from her own imagination is rocket fuel for a woman's sexual pleasure. Drag it out a bit and be playful with her submission. When a man dominates a woman, she gets highly aroused. That is the way a woman's body was designed. A man's masculine frame is the greatest foreplay. It puts a woman in the mood throughout the day and primes her for wanting sex. This frame of dominance is what women masturbate to in their dominance-erotica. A man doesn't have to be a billionaire playboy with a mansion to give his woman pleasure, all he needs is a dominant frame and the confidence to use it. Be her fantasy by fucking her the way you want to fuck her without showing doubt or fear. It is a man's certainty of what he wants that increases a woman's sexual satisfaction. Frame is needed to sell sex. A man must be confident and assertive in his wants and desires.

A man bonds with a woman by her accepting his dirty mind as normal. The intimacy is through the shared secret of his unique sexuality. If man is not expressing his true dirty mind with his woman, then he is too frightened by judgment of his sexual self. This cowardice prevents him from having sexual intimacy and fulfilment. A man needs to act on his dirty fantasies with his woman for them to draw closer. *A woman's orgasm lays upon dirt.* It is through the abandonment of sexual anxiety that a man reassures his woman of his confidence. Be brave in acting out the fantasies that have built up throughout the day.

Every aspect of sex should be dominance play from a man to a woman. When a woman wants to dominate a man sexually, it comes about from her desire to dominate him in the entire relationship.

Sometimes a man will be disrespected by a woman and in a passive aggressive way he will still engage in sex. This is known as a "hate fuck." Hate fucking is falling into the woman's frame and is self-hatred. A man must get respect always before sex. He engages in rough sex not because he is provoked but because he wants to. There could be an innate reason why a woman would disrespect a man in order to get rough sex. As if she is rattling the tiger's cage because she herself wants to see a tiger in action. This could be from her being with a weak man whom she must inspire to have balls. But nothing is worse for the masculine spirit more than passive aggressively take-out anger on a woman during sex. All rough sex should be rational, not emotional.

A woman needs to be trained to enjoy giving blowjobs. If a man helps a woman to enjoy blowjobs, then she will crave them for her own pleasure.

"But Jerr," a voice calls out from outside the page, "How does a man help a woman enjoy blowjobs?"

Two ways. First a man should view a blowjob as more of a *blowgift* he is giving to his woman. If a man takes confident pleasure in sticking his dick in his woman's mouth, she will share the same frame-of-thought. Second, he must train her to associate his cock-in-her-mouth with her own sexual pleasure. This can be done with Pavlovian conditioning. When a man is giving his woman clitoral pleasure, (with vibration or fingering) he should have his cock in her mouth, if she is about to orgasm, he should place his cock in her mouth. With enough sessions she will begin to associate cock-in-the-mouth with her own sexual pleasure.

Be the dominant leader she craves and wants to submit to. Make her do things that are "dirty" that you spent the entire day thinking about. That is what she expects from a framed man. And a man should remember that women do not resent specific sex acts, they resent the weakness in bad attempts at sex acts. They resent all sex from unframed men but especially dominant sex with them. Dominant sex must come from a dominant frame. If an unframed man attempts dominance, a woman will laugh and then resent him during the act. For a man to improve his sex life, first he must work on his masculine frame otherwise it will backfire on him in the bedroom.

Premature ejaculation comes from over reactivity to the woman's frame. But before I write more about this, first we must define it. Premature ejaculation is when a man comes before he wants to. *That is the definition.* It is not when a man orgasms before the woman achieves orgasm. Whenever a man chooses to cum is the correct time. If it is twenty minutes, then it is twenty minutes. If it is ten minutes, then it is ten minutes. If it is five minutes, then it is five minutes. That is the man's decision, and a man doesn't always want to last long. Sometimes we have more important things to do and prefer quick sex. Men who want to have sex for a long time are usually men who are afraid of female dissatisfaction. These men have weak frames and are controlled by fear. A man sets the timetable of the sex act and does not show doubt in himself during or after. Even if a man did become reactive to a woman's stimuli and ejaculates faster than he wanted, he walks away as if it was planned. Otherwise, he projects weakness, and this is seen as pathetic by the woman. Never show weakness after sex. She does not want to deal with a man's insecurities after sex. Always exit in confidence.

How does a man last longer? He must control his stimulated state. He should not overly stimulate himself with pornography and when having sex, he must focus the mind outside what most excites him. Also, he should focus his mind on other parts of his own body outside his own penis and hands. These will help him to control his reactivity to over stimulus.

A woman should always be louder during sex. If a man is louder than a woman, he breaks his frame. If a woman is too loud, it is dominance and must be stifled. All moaning from a woman is a biological shit test to get the man to prematurely ejaculate. Did you think shit tests ever end? If she tries to direct sex, stick a couple fingers in her mouth to quiet her down.

"But Jerr," a voice comes from outside the book, "That sounds rude and disrespectful to women."

Read erotica for women. There is not a whole lot of respect going on in those books, its kind of like, and call me crazy but... it's kind of like a woman gets sexually aroused by being "disrespected."

"But Jerr," the voice interrupts, "That is just because some women have broken psychologies."

Wrong. All sex is an act of disrespect to a woman's body in some degree. A bee disrespects a flower when it tramples on it and a man disrespects a woman by penetrating her with his penis. The act itself is an intrusion into a woman's space by the man. A woman feels she is being disrespected only because modern women have been trained by feminism to view all submission as humiliation. This ideology has corrupted many women's minds to hate sex. Feminism has created more sexual dysfunction than anything else on the planet. The key to healthy sex is to not be afraid of desecrating a woman's "dignity" in small ways. Women's erotica can teach a man how to "desecrate" his woman for her own pleasure. This grows within an established relationship between two people who trust each other. A man shouldn't attempt overly dominant sex with a woman too early if his frame is weak.

Unframed men (and some weak framed men) will empower their daughters to feminism because they fear their sexual surrender. They want to create another dominant woman in the world because they have sex anxiety. This is arrogant in them wanting to control their daughters' innate pleasure while also equally self-loathing to their own gender. Men should not think about the sex of the women in their family. Fucking is as natural and healthy as breathing. It is not abuse and it is not cruel. To fuck is to understand human nature. Each man must overcome his sex anxiety.

The closer a man gets to overcoming his false-holy image of women, the closer a man will get to pleasing his woman sexually. She is not an angel or god, she is a woman and women like to be fucked.

The

wall

makes

her

fetch

The wall is slow and relaxed which allows the woman to fall into her hummingbird energy. A woman, when she is in her feminine, naturally buzzes around her framed man. Why? Because throughout generations of ancestral learning women have adapted to this behavior. For millennia, men would be gone most the day hunting resources to bring back to the woman who was home with children. When ancient man got home, he would rest his weary bones and the woman would buzz around him in servitude. Modern day woman still has this feminine energy to her. Even when a man and woman both work equally, a woman will still buzz about with womanly chores. If a woman doesn't do this it is because she has become masculinized. Every dirty house tends to have a fat dominant woman inside.

This innate quality to feminine nature makes a woman feel like a female. If the man were buzzing about doing domestic chores while the woman was watching TV, the man would be in his feminine and the woman in her masculine. Those type of relationships have severe sexual dysfunction which proves that a progressive attitude has yet to bring dignity to the man and sex to the bedroom. A progressive relationship will never succeed because a progressive relationship is based on stripping the man of authority and granting the woman his power. That destroys a man's dignity, and nothing brings more sexual pleasure to a woman than a man with a king's dignity. Even dominant women will talk about wanting a "king" in their lives. But a king must have authority, or he is merely a puppet. If a woman refuses to give reverence and authority to her man, then she refuses her man his kingship. When a framed man doesn't feel like a king in a relationship, he will abandon the woman who disrespects him to find one that does. An unframed man is used to humiliation and will continue his relationship with passive aggression and self-loathing like a jester who plots to poison his queen's chalice.

A man's authority in his relationship only exists if the woman proves it through obedience. And obedience only exists if a man is brave enough to request it in the first place.

The thing most unframed men do not understand is that a woman bonds through obedience. She bonds through servitude to her leader. Think about it like this. If a leader makes zero requests, how is he showing authority?

Make requests of her.

A man, if he genuinely loves a woman, will summon the courage to tell her to make him a sandwich. This will prove that she is submissive and wants to care for him like her ancestral DNA is telling her to. This is known as the Benjamin

Franklin effect, the more someone does a favor for someone, the more familiar and less resistant they will become in their attitude towards future giving. Requests build a relationship between leader and follower. A man can use this in his business with his employees or in his relationship with his woman. To be a king, a man must make demands on his woman.

"But Jerr," a voice calls out from off the page, "I don't like bossing people around."

To be a leader a man must summon courage to boss.

"But Jerr," a voice calls out from off the page, "I followed your advice and asked my woman to do me a favor. Right after she asked me to do a favor for her, is that okay?"

That is not submission, that is equality. To be a king is to ask a favor of others and to be able to refuse favors. Sound rude? Maybe it is, maybe all authority is rude in a sense, but that is how it works. The reason a man should feel comfortable having authority over his woman has nothing to do with anything beyond that they are in a relationship and he is her man. My woman should not be obedient to me because I'm Jerr, she should be obedient to me because I am a man just like you. We are men and our women are beneath us in authority. And if they do not like being obedient then we replace them with other women who would be willing to treat us like kings. Remember a man commands and a woman either rejects his leadership or follows. If she follows, then she is in her feminine and therefore attractive to us. If she doesn't follow our direction, then she disrespects our authority and becomes unattractive to us. A woman who doesn't believe in our kingship is a woman wanting a different kingdom. A woman who doesn't believe her man to be a king only has that mindset because she knows her man to be a jester. What man would want to live with that level of disbelief pouring over him, day in and day out? He would have to be full of self-hatred. A man should be increasing his masculine dignity little by little every day he is alive until he stops breathing.

"But Jerr," a voice calls out from off the page, "I have a horrible imagination and don't know what to ask her to do."

Start small. Ask her to get you a beer or if you don't drink alcohol, a sparkling water. No sparkling water? Ask her to go to the store and buy you some and then ask her to put in the fridge. Wait until it is chilled then ask her to get you a cold sparkling water. This is relationship therapy and submission training. It builds her love for you.

"But Jerr," a voice calls out from off the page, "I asked her to do all that and she looked mad at me the whole time."

That is because she doesn't respect your masculine frame. She must see you as weak and your frame as weak. She needs to get used to submission and her resentment in being submissive will subside. If it does not subside, then that means she cannot get over the fact that a jester is trying to be a king. In that case my suggestion would be to end the relationship.

"But Jerr--"

Let me finish. A man must make further demands on a woman's body to reassure him of her loyalty and submission. The reason goes beyond the Benjamin Franklin effect and goes straight into the heart of a man's desire. A man who gets his own way is highly valued in women. If a man doesn't fight for his own desire, then who will? Maybe a man will summon the balls to ask for his desires sometime before he is put into the ground. When his body starts to turn into something resembling kimchi maybe then he will finally ask for what he wants.

If a woman is too fat, ask her to lose weight. If a woman's hair is too long or too short then tell her what you want. It can be as simple as a man liking blue and him asking his woman to wear more blue outfits. She performs to the beat of your drum. Make demands of her and let her prove herself to you. Don't be obsessive about it but make it clear how she can please you though her actions and let her surprise you.

Listen to women long enough and they all speak about wanting strong leaders and kings in their relationships. They speak truth but don't want to give up authority. Usually, a real dominant woman will talk about wanting a king or being in a relationship with her "king" before following it up with a quick "and I'm his queen."

Never trust a woman who calls herself a queen. If she calls her man a "king" before calling herself a "queen" is a shiny way to say "equality."

A woman craves dominance but also fears surrender. It comes from lacking trust in men. But when it comes to you, she should respect and trust your authority. Why? Because either she believes in you or you give her an opportunity to believe in another guy. Life is challenging for everyone and nobody is guaranteed a thing. I learned this when I got cheated on and my retirement plans melted before me.

Now I make demands known or I make myself known to another woman. Life is just too short to be with a woman who doesn't trust or respect her leader. A man deserves better because his masculine pride matters. That is the key to the kingdom. That is what makes a king. A man who believes in his masculine pride and makes a woman share that same belief. When a woman obeys a man, what she is telling him is she respects his authority and BELIEVES in his leadership. She BELIEVES in him. This is what makes a woman as precious as a rare jewel, her belief in her man. Women who do not believe in the men they are in relationships with are hidden rebels waiting to defect to another kingdom. They hold bitter resentment in their heart and will use a man's dignity as a bridge to another man's castle. That is why it is important to have her prove her love through her respect and obedience. If she doesn't respect, she doesn't love and if she doesn't love then she should be abandoned for a true love who follows commands.

When I was unframed, I remember seeing men boss their women around and used to think that the women must have had resentment for these men. After living some life, I can say with a certainty that women resent the men who don't ask. Because those commanding men understood female nature better than me and were helping their women fall into their feminine.

It is up to the man to help a woman feel like a woman. Without a masculine man a woman is forced into a begrudging dominance. Women want dominance but resent the power as soon as it's in their hands. That is the vicious cycle of society and civilization; women craving power and then becoming resentful over its responsibility. Over and over and over again. The cruel nature of the universe is that weak men allow dominant women to create a society full of decay before a collapse which resets it back to the strong man submissive woman dynamic. It is like a tower up into the sky that wobbles because it has become feminized in rot. It leans and sways from being top heavy in irrational emotion. Sometimes it takes failure of female leadership in a feminized society to bring about the end of a civilization. But if men want to save their civilization, they must be willing to take power from women and give it back to men. That is the way a society stabilizes itself from its feminine chaos.

Modern times are not the only gender fluid times. It has been happening over and over for millennia. When a civilization becomes rich, it becomes debauched and feminized which begins its decay. Whether it was ancient Greece, Rome or Modern western civilization.

If you want to save your relationship and save your civilization, ask your woman to make you a sandwich.

PLACE YOUR PRIDE ABOVE YOUR WOMAN'S PRIDE

The

wall

does

not

react

A woman will tell a man to "just be yourself" while rewarding another man who overcomes his weaknesses. Women will tell men to express themselves while rewarding men who have a framed non-expression. A woman's eternal advice regardless of context "be more like me." By now my reader should be wise enough not to listen to a woman's words but to only pay attention to a woman's actions. If a woman rewards your behavior with respect and sex then keep doing it otherwise change your behavior until she starts to reward you.

One element of masculinity that a woman rewards is when a man is non-reactionary. This is a discipline and does not come natural to most men. It takes practice and work. Unframed men get confused about this when they see a framed man talking to a woman. They will see the man just nodding and the woman seeming a bit nervous as she over talks. The unframed man thinks that the framed man is making the woman uncomfortable with his non-expression. To an unframed man a woman appearing a bit nervous is a cruelty. If she were talking to him, he would talk just as much, he would express just as much in order to reassure her and to calm her nerves. Unframed men believe that by showing their own nerves is a reassurance to females. They want to show a woman that they too lack confidence which they hope will build a peer-to-peer relationship. What they don't know is that a man who appears nervous only makes a woman more nervous.

Unframed men know little of a woman's nature. When a woman is in her feminine, she will have a soft buzz to her presence. Her soft buzz is from her arousal. It is the walled presence of a framed man that calms a woman's anxiety and inspires this "soft buzz."

"But Jerr," a voice comes from outside the book, "Why would a woman be calmed by being nervous?"

She is nervous because she is in qualification mode to the man and his non-expression is what calms her down under his frame. When a woman is talking to a man who uses less expression this allows a woman to expand her ego and this ego expansion is what makes a woman feel a connection. A framed man's walled countenance is like a white wall that a woman's film of imagination projects on to. Women value their imagination more than reality. A woman creates the image, and the framed man allows her to place the image upon his blank masculine slate.

"But Jerr," a voice calls out from outside the page, "But isn't that just an illusion for the woman.... And doesn't the man want to express his real personality. Doesn't he feel lonely behind the wall?"

Real is boring. A woman is like a magician who cast spells upon herself. Love is self-enchantment. Her imagination is the most precious possession she has, and she wants to be possessed by it. A framed man allows her to use her imagination which allows her to use her intuition to unpack what the wall thinks. Both are important to a woman's sexual arousal. When an unframed man pours out every little detail about himself, it robs himself of mystery and the woman of her fantasy. The wall sets the frame of who qualifies to whom. If an unframed man is nervously speaking to a silent woman, he will be falling into a jester mode. But when a man keeps his wall up, this allows him to be in his king mode. When a man's wall is strong, a woman will happily qualify to him and happily fall into her feminine frame. The whole time a woman talks before a walled man she is thinking "What is he thinking?" and after they part ways, she will ponder more about him and what he thought about her. This cycle of thinking further builds a woman's interest in his mystery. Why? Because her self-made narrative is forcing her to increase her investment in the framed man. He didn't need to talk because the woman talked for him in her own mind. She did all the footwork for her own arousal.

When an unframed man narrates line-by-line every detail of why a woman should fall in love with him, he kills the mystery and arrogantly robs a woman of building her own narrative. Unframed men, although they may not know it, are the most ignorant and arrogant men alive. Maybe that is why women so harshly punish and exploit them. When unframed men try to talk their way into a pussy or try to buy a woman's affection with gifts, it only signals to the woman that they are confused sexually and thereby easy targets to exploit. This allows a woman to enjoy her walled sex and if the framed man doesn't want a relationship, she can settle for an unframed man to rule over. Women feel little guilt in exploiting unframed men because unframed men resemble women in behavior and women are cruel to each other. Unframed men tend to use gifts obsessively which is a type of exploitation. It shows that the man has low self-esteem, and that he views sex as transactional as if the woman were a prostitute to him. How degrading for a woman to feel that material possession was what her love was based on.

When men start picking up frame at first, their walls become rigid as if they are attempting an impersonation of Terminator. This ultra-non-reaction is awkward and projects weakness. Why? Because the more control a man has over something the more, he can balance between the two extremes in moderation. For example, while abstinence is the best solution for some alcoholics, moderation is a true sign of strength. Abstinence is only a final solution when a man's addiction is overwhelming to his self-control, so he sides on the healthy extreme instead of the unhealthy extreme. The same can be said of a man's walled countenance. Being overly expressive signals a lack of discipline and control. Being overly rigid signals that the man only knows masculinity with the IQ of a caveman. Women are smart enough to understand intelligence in men. A man's mastery over his expression comes from reading other people's faces in interaction when he's practicing frame. (An online generation of men would have difficulty with this.) What a man needs to understand with facial expression is that a little goes a long way. A smirk says more from a framed man than a shit eating grin from an unframed man. The smirk says whatever a woman's imagination wants it to say, it barely even registers on the man's face but already a woman has written a novel on it. She knows exactly what is means, in fact only she truly knows what it means. (Women think arrogantly like this.)

When a man's working on his non-expression and doesn't want to veer into robot territory, he should imagine what an amused stone looks like. That is what his wall should be, like an amused stone. Why amused? Because amused is a micro expression that projects confidence and contentment. A woman needs to know with small gestures that a man is genuinely enjoying himself behind his wall and that he is not comatose.

If a man holds back over expression and focuses on micro expression, then he will start to notice a woman paying more attention to his facial features. Why? Because she is trying to unpack what is going on behind the man's wall. The wall is the most fun thing in the world for a woman's intuition and that is why she will reward the wall with gifts like respect and sex. She gives a wall whatever the hell the wall wants because the wall provides back so much in return for her feminine pleasure.

So much positive reaction can come from a man's non-reaction. Beyond just the sexual stimulant that a woman gets from a man's wall, the wall also signifies security to her. Non-reaction represents calm because a stressful environment creates a body that reacts with gestures of anxiety. When a man is startled or scared, his body will shake in fear and if a woman is looking for a protector, she will avoid easily startled men. The stillness of a man's walled presence calms a woman under his certainty-of-safety. This appearance of her leader reassures the woman and allows her to think about something other than an invading barbarian or a crouching wolf at the cave's entrance in her ancestral mind. Within the frame of her safety that her protector prides, thoughts of sex can blossom forth.

An unframed man with his nervous overtalking and anxious expressions signals to women that they both are about to die. *How romantic of him.* By being calm a man allows the woman to think about something other than immediate danger.

Women get anxious around a framed man when his wall is too rigid. They try to read his reassurance of safety but his non-expression is too unreadable. That is why it is important for framed men to work on positive micro expressions like the "amused stone."

Some dominant women end up with rigid stone type guys who let their assertive women narrate everything in their relationships. With these women, the rigid stones let them expand their ego further by letting them interpret everything from their imagination. Maybe the entire relationship is all in their imagination?

"But Jerr," a voice calls out from outside the page, "All this talk about micro expressions and amused stones is making me depressed... isn't there more to life than hiding behind a wall?"

Is there anything more to life besides respect and sex? Is nervous giggling and wide-eyed looks of fear so hard to give up? When men have ventured through "Unframed Valley" and experienced its sandstorms of disrespect with memory of its severe sexual droughts, they would never speak ill of the wall. The wall is the land of sexual plenty with bountiful respect. The wall hides the promised land just as walls surrounded Eden. That is why a man practices micro expressions and speaks of "amused stone" In an imperfect world, we choose the lesser of two evils.

At first when a man starts picking up his masculine frame, he will feel some despair as if he is destroying his emotional security blanket by giving up the constant validation of expression. Because when a man builds his entire personality around expression it will be a challenge to stifle the familiarity of himself. The practice of non-expression becomes easier with time but there are things to remember when dealing with emotional control of a walled experience. Lifting weights helps emotional regulation and helps to "express a man" when he feels stuck inside himself. Also avoiding needless media that incites depressing feelings can be a help. If a man drinks all day, doesn't exercise and listens to sad music, he will be challenged more than he needs to be.

When women start rewarding men sexually for talking too much and start respecting men who lack emotional control, then we won't need books like this to help men. The only reason I am writing this book is because so many men are getting left behind because they lacked a father figure in their lives. I've been there, it is a real rough existence and so I hope to spare other men of the pain of having their masculine pride trampled upon. If they can get laid, then good but that is not why I write. I write because men have been forgotten in this generation of single mothers and absent fathers and are being exploited for their ignorance. I hope to empower men, not like a pickup artist who helps men to increase notch counts like mindless animals, but rather because I want every man to be most dignified in his reality on the planet. Modern man must take away authority from his woman in his relationship because modern women have too much control in our current society. This generation of forgotten men must empower themselves and start commanding the authority that was thrown into the hands of these entitled women. When every man becomes the king of his relationship, feminism will fade away. That is my hope for the sake of masculine dignity and for all mankind.

The

wall

believes

To be a man is to view the self as a transcendence of reality and not a victim of reality. This masculine view is how men have mustered the bravery needed to venture into unexplored territory since the beginning. Boldness requires belief. Self-belief is like a wall in a pool that a swimmer uses to propel himself forward from. Without belief the spirit sinks into doubt.

A father gives the gift of belief to a boy whereas a mother instills doubt to cradle him in safety. Women are ruled by anxiety and fear. They keep boys in tight safety nets which robs them of self-belief. In no other time has young men been coddled to such a degree from a mother's fear of their potential harm. These young boys are kept in sight always from womanly paranoia. It has been the father's job for countless millennia to separate the mother from the boy in order to establish independence. The father reassures the mother of the boy's strength against the surrounding environment. He instills self-belief in the boy to overcome reality and his mother's fears. When the boy falls, he holds the mother back so the boy will be able to stand without help. The father knows that internal belief is what will carry the boy into unknown futures that they will not be able to protect him from. This wisdom has been stolen from a forgotten generation of fatherless men. These men have been given nothing but womanly fear. And that is why they prefer safety above risk, comfort above adventure and fantasy above reality. They let fear and doubt rule their minds while they place their belief in others.

What unframed men must realize is that the emotional dependency that their mothers instilled in them came with a steep price of disbelief. The more a boy relied on his mother to ease his fear, the weaker he became in solving his own problems. When a woman is separated from her man, she will have increased fear and doubt. She will then depend on her boys more for her own mental wellbeing and encourage their dependency to reassure her. This mother-son relationship is like two people hugging when they should be swimming. The mother does this from her own weak emotional frame and cannot help it. That is why men are essential in the psychological upbringing of boys. They separate the love embrace which allows the boys to achieve the self-belief that the mother is preventing with her emotional support.

This forgotten generation is a generation of disbelievers. They exist in doubt about their impact on reality and see themselves as helpless victims before it.

"But Jerr," a voice calls out from outside the page, "I'm not a momma's boy. I just need to make sure that she is okay every day."

Distance yourself from her. A man raised by a single mother must push her away for the greater good of them both. He needs to emotionally detach himself from her frame of authority and be okay with the distance necessary for his own emotional autonomy. Many men struggle with this cold view because they lacked the rational mind from their father. The father understands distance and detachment. Not because he is cruel or a monster but because he understands the importance of confidence of self. And only through detachment can confidence blossom. That is why men need to free themselves from the emotional support that keeps them stagnant and small. It is from the void of self that belief springs forth. Be okay with separation and reassure others that they will be okay separated. This allows healthy belief to grow in between the measured space.

Men suffer when they emotionally depend on others because it is a woman's game. That is why mothers will encourage emotional dependence of their sons. They do not want to give up their power over them because they are controlled by fear of loss. When a man picks up frame and pushes his mother away, he sets healthy boundaries for his own mother's emotional being. She doesn't know it, that is why a man must teach her the correct path. This allows him to be able to achieve the emotional detachment needed for his own wellbeing. The detachment that a good father would have taught him to have. A leader must rely only on himself for validation. This takes independent thought and will. This takes self-belief.

The

wall

needs

belief

When an unframed man speaks his woman will often roll her eyes. Why? Because this action signals her resentment and lack of trust in his authority. She wants it to be clear for others that she does not believe in him. Women with unframed men do not believe their men's words and especially do not trust their men's authority. They cannot get over the doubt they have for their men because their men inspire doubt with their bodies and speech.

When a man has a wall up this tells the world "believe my speech" and women agree to those terms because a walled existence is highly disciplined with control and forethought. It is not like the "speak first, think later" approach that many women and unframed men use. A framed man's speech signals that he has thought twice before uttering his words. And when he speaks, he uses only the bare minimum of words necessary to clarify his point. He does have a point and that is a powerful thing. He doesn't ramble on with half thoughts. He has built up a reputation of using words that do not inspire doubt and does not talk needlessly.

When a framed man speaks, he gets less disrespectful eyes rolls of disbelief from his woman because his woman believes his speech. Isn't that a glorious thing? When a woman has sincere belief in her man, she fills him with pride. She believes in his authority because he has worked hard in earning it unlike an unframed man who demands to be respected because he "says so" (unframed men when they become dominant fall into tyranny because their followers have more doubt that needs to be controlled) instead of working hard to inspire submission.

To have leadership over a woman, a man's speech must be trusted. If a man tells a woman to do something, he will get resistance only because she doubts his authority. She is full of doubt in him and does not believe he is a leader. That is why disrespect is so hurtful to the masculine spirit. Because disrespect from a woman is an act of disbelief in his leadership. And if a man is not leading, he is dying. To be a man and not a leader in a relationship is a humiliation with great suffering. Not just because following a woman is dreadful but because women themselves punish follower-men with severity. Remove the authority from a man and you remove his spirit. He might as well exist as an impotent eunuch shuffling around under a woman's ever rolling eyes. Women make horrible leaders over men in relationships because they cannot control their tyranny. Only when a framed man leads in his relationship does everyone align with nature. The more dominant women in society, the more hidden humiliation exists behind closed doors. Feminism and the weak men who allowed it, have decimated the masculine spirit for generations of men. It is up to this modern generation of men to regain the power of their voices and to use them in being the rational leaders they were born to be. This begins by a man empowering his speech and recognizing that a woman who doubts his speech is acting like a negative cheerleader. Why would a man want to come home to a woman who is rooting for him to fail? This behavior is relationship ending. A woman must respect her man's speech as authority or another woman will. There is not a relationship without a woman's belief in her man's authority.

The

wall

is

distant

    A leader respects his own emotional and physical space, and his follower shares the same thought. By now in the book, you realize the logic of a man setting a *frame of thought* and if the man's belief is strong enough, the woman will share it. If a man believes his attention has value, then the woman will also think his attention has value. Like most things in life rarity increases value and this applies to a man's availability. The more available a man makes himself to his woman the less appreciation he will get in return. When a man measures out his boundaries, he lets those around him know that he values himself. Unframed men become unframed because they feel obligated to pour themselves out for their women. To them, holding back is rude and giving forth is virtuous. People who exploit them and do not respect them create deep anger in these men because of their self-viewed virtue. "I pour forth so why shouldn't others do the same?" Sounds like irrational hopeful logic. It's not based on how anything gains value in real life, rarity makes value. The more something exists in commonality the less people treasure it. And that is the key to a framed man's view of himself, he wants people to treasure his availability and not take it for granted.

One of the most certain things in life is how quickly people become entitled to something given freely. Someone becoming entitled is to be expected when no boundaries are established, and framed men know this. In a woman's mind she only wants to be with someone who values himself more than he values her. By limiting attention to a woman, a man increases his own value before her eyes. A woman is happiest when she can reach out to a walled man and there is enough space in between for her to do so freely. If a man makes himself overly available and never pulls his attention away from his woman, it will make her feel trapped with a low value man's desperation. This feeling of entrapment prevents a woman from having the emotional space needed for arousal. And when a woman feels entrapped, she will be overwhelmed with the compulsion for flight.

This comes from a few different reasons. In a woman's ancestral memory, she has been trained to be separated from her man most of the day from back when men hunted and the women were left with the children. Often men had to be on the hunt for days if not weeks or longer. This coding is deep in women and applies even to modern times. A woman likes a man who doesn't hang around and who has a life of his own. Distance has been a masculine trait since the dawn of time. Modern man lacks the essential distance needed to please his woman. A man going to work is a form of distance, but it might not be enough. Playing basketball after work with friends is distance but it might not be enough. Every woman is different, and some require more distance than others. Figuring out the needed amount for a specific woman takes observance and effort.

"But Jerr," a voice calls out from off the page, "My girl and I work together, and I don't have any friends to play basketball with...how do I establish distance?"

If a man cannot supply physical distance then he needs to increase his emotional distance. Distance is distance. By pulling back emotional validation from a woman this allows her the space to pine. And pining for her man is what a woman wants to do. A woman cannot pine for something that won't leave her the hell alone. "Absence makes the heart fonder" is one of the truest sayings on earth and nothing makes a woman's heart flutter about like a physically and emotionally absent man. The way a man can decrease his emotional availability is to ignore a woman and concern himself with anything around him but her. The goal is to ignore her which creates *emotional space.* It can be as simple as reading a book by me. This distraction of attention deprives a woman of validation. Women crave validation by nature to help them ease the anxiety of their emotions. That is why women talk about feelings. So, they don't have to feel alone on their emotional journey. They need company to reassure them of their own existence. A man reassures himself of his own existence which pulls the emotionally needy little creature into orbit. The more a man ignores a woman, the more he elevates himself above her which arouses her attention. In her mind she thinks who is this beast that ignores my holy presence? Most unframed men need to realize that deflating a woman's ego is what summons her orgasm, not inflating it. This does not mean a man should insult a woman only that he should value his attention above her. This alone will deflate her ego to normal levels and build attraction for him. This holding back of attention is what draws her in. This could be as simple as not texting back right away or not answering her speech right away. A man could count to three before verbal response to trigger this. Unframed men are overreactive in general, but they tend to respond too quickly to women which lowers the value of their attention. A man's non-reaction increases a woman's reaction, and a woman tends to rationalize her reaction, as necessary. If she is spinning her wheels for instance over a guy this means the man is dominating her thoughts. It's like the saying "all publicity is good publicity."

This distance that a framed man provides for a woman is fuel for her best friend. Know what that is already? *Her imagination.* Nobody on the planet is a greater thief of imagination than an unframed man. Romance can only blossom from a woman's mind.

Another reason a man needs to establish distance is this reassures his woman that he does not need her. This is important in a relationship because nothing builds more resentment in a woman than a man who is dependent upon her.

"But Jerr," a voice calls out from off the page, "How can a woman feel that I am dependent on her by just making myself available to her?"

Because she knows the more available a man is the less options he has and the less options he has the more dependent on her being his one option she will be. And she is correct. Distance allows a man to establish that he is not emotionally dependent. This reassures a woman because in her ancestral memory she needs a man to take care of reality and not be crying when he should be killing dinner. Since women are emotional creatures, if a man becomes emotionally needy it is as if he climbs on top of her while she swims through the giant waves of her own emotional chaos. Sound overwhelming? It is and that is why men need to take their emotional distance seriously. The wall reassures because the wall stands strong regardless of her internal turmoil. A man should be the rational anchor against his woman's ocean of emotion.

Most dopamine is released in the brain in the anticipation phase prior to reward and a man's distance creates the space needed for a woman to build her own dopamine hit. Romance and attraction are based on this out-of-the-hand approach like a carrot before a horse. By measuring out reward and by keeping it out of reach, a man inflames a woman's passion. When a man keeps his attention just out of his woman's reach, he keeps her interested and coming back for more. This measured approach is the opposite of an unframed man. He is unmeasured and unrestrained. He thinks just giving a woman whatever she desires will create value for him. Ignorance and arrogance.

I've seen unframed men in relationships that think by applying the "happy wife, happy life" maxim will increase their women's contentment. That only feeds the beast of a woman's ego and discontentment. Nothing on the planet can compare to the pure villainy of a woman's inflated ego. It is a black hole of dissatisfaction and arrogant self-entitlement. A woman doesn't need a man to give her what she asks, she needs a man to know when to tell her "NO." And nothing pleases a woman more than a man with the balls to say "NO" to her. When a man cannot say "NO" to a woman, she will see this as fraudulent cowardice that deserves exploitation. That is why these unframed men become abused under these women's dominance. *Weak men create Jezebels.* They feed the beast that will eventually consume them and so why should the woman pity such a fool? To exist as a woman is already challenging enough without worrying about a man's foolishness.

When a woman's ego has been fed by weak men, she will have psychological disorders. These women will attempt to crush all who dare oppose them. They feel self-hatred deep down and want to escape the weak men that created their own villainy. That is why a cruel and dominant woman will seek a masculine frame that will save her from herself. Women desire a rational man who has the balls to put them in their place. That is why women cheat on these unframed men with framed men. These women are searching for the cure to their own wickedness. They do not want to be with weak men who allow them to be unruly. They want to be feminine and submissive because that heals them of tyranny. They want to be under a dominant man's frame to not only protect themselves of the reality of life but also the reality of themselves. They want to be sanctified by being denied. They want the sexual arousal of a man brave enough to stand up to them. That is what these weak men are too afraid to admit, that a woman is pleased by what is kept away from her. The out-of-the-hand approach. It is the leader's hand that keeps them on the feminine path and helps them control their own egos. It is under his frame that they are reassured and subdued. They want to be calmed by masculine order. That is why framed men build the wall and keep them out. We do it for their own benefit because we know feminine nature and know what fires of hell exist in a woman's psyche when she gains power over us.

A man who keeps what his woman wants the most out of her reach, keeps her chasing her own desire. Many women and unframed men think that framed men are emotionally neglectful and therefore emotional abusers. It is not emotional abuse but rather a deep understanding of a woman's emotional need for neglect. When a framed man pulls his attention away from a woman is a caring and rational act.

WOMANKIND IS MERELY

BACKGROUND NOISE TO

THE POWER OF

MASCULINE FRAME

The

snake

in

the

walled

garden

In the garden of Eden, the earliest mother was deceived by the snake in the tree of knowledge of good and evil. The education of Eve is what made her forget her righteous state of submission within a man's frame. Her increased wisdom over Adam led them both into a mother complex which compelled Adam's fall from his own grace by casting him into her feminine frame of authority. Eve's expanded ego was overwhelming to Adam who forgot himself and followed her out from Eden without his masculine dignity, like a child.

Just as a snake can make its way past a garden's wall, the same is true of a woman's intelligence to a man's masculine frame. Feminine intelligence can flip any man's frame. It slides underneath and undermines authority. That is why intellectuals are the first rounded up and executed under an authoritarian regime change. Why? Because intelligence is like a snake in the garden to authority. It eventually undermines the current power structure.

The current feminist society that encourages feminine intelligence is undermining the natural sexual selection of our species.

"But Jerr," a voice calls out from off the page, "Are you saying that a woman should not be allowed to read and write?"

Of course not. What I am saying is that mankind should be more educated than womankind for everyone's benefit. If a woman has a certain level of education, then the man should be encouraged to have more so. A woman's education is not the real threat, it is the comparable education of man that undermines himself. That is why a man should educate himself as much as he can to avoid the frame issues that he will have in a relationship with a modern woman. Each modern feminist is a partaker of the forbidden fruit of her expanded mind. She rises in ambition only to suffer sexual dysfunction in her romance because men have not been equally groomed of their own ambition. This framework of empowering women over men is foolish and arrogant to the natural order of our sex. Modern parents laud their daughter's academic accolades while forgetting their sons to video games. This forgotten generation of men has been abandoned to fantasy while women are empowered to reality.

When a woman is more intelligent than her man, she will speak truthfully of matters that are perceived to him to be a shit test. This increased "false alarm" in the simpler man will cause friction of authority because the woman knows he leads bullheadedly. Even when the simpler man recognizes his woman's truth this will only inflate her ego as he is forced into a backseat to decision-making. His lack of education will cause him to fall behind her in capacity for leadership. She will naturally assume authority from her overwhelming intelligence and undermine his masculine wall. This is not the fault of the woman as much it is a fault of how our societies are organized to empower women. The feminist movement is a movement of suffering, low birth rates and increased feminine anxiety because it is a war on our sexual selection.

This knowledge of relationship friction is known to feminist supporters. From their fear of its romantic failures, they work at making men fetishize their own emasculation by gaslighting them into viewing it as "enlightenment". This can be likened to making a slave love his chains in order to make the plantation operate. But even when the man loves his own chains-of-emasculation within the mother-child dynamic of feminist romance, the sex always dies out under feminine control. And when the sex withers, the relationship dies. The feminist movement has failed countless couples' sexuality, yet they continue to try to give breath to the beast like a reanimation of Frankenstein's monster. Let it die and let us all move on in alignment with the natural-order-of-things. A man as leader over his wife and children. This arrangement is how our bodies and minds adapted over countless millennia as it complements our ancestral memory. Womankind emotionally need and sexually desire a stronger mankind. That is why society should groom young men as natural born leaders. It doesn't mean that a society should encourage women to be barefoot illiterates, rather it means that the education of womankind comes at a price depending on the how they encourage the men in their society for education.

"But Jerr," a voice calls out from off the page, "My woman is wicked smart. She is a real genius, and I must take a back seat to many matters. How can I make it work?"

She must accept your authority even at cost of failure. The man's frame of authority must be strong enough to lead his woman into unknown pastures. For example, if a woman is dominant and intelligent then she could very well get a career opportunity that she will deem essential for moving. If the man follows along to her career ambition because his job is less prestigious, he will set the frame of her authority. This would cause the man to join the woman's world.

A man should never follow a woman towards her dreams, and he should never join a woman's world. That destroys his own masculine frame as he becomes a dependent along her journey. And a woman will punish his dependency as weakness which will eventually unravel the relationship. There is nothing a woman despises and resents more than a man who depends on her. That is why a man should view his work, even if it makes less money than his woman's work as more prestigious. She abandons her dreams and stays in a man's world because she loves her man even if it doesn't make financial sense. If he follows her, she will fall out of love quick anyhow. The only real option for true romance is the woman following the man. If a man is in a scenario as described then he should make the woman decide her own fate within the relationship. She goes and leaves the relationship or she stays and chooses love over ambition. That choice will set the frame for her respecting the man's world as greater. And the man's world, even if less educated, less prestigious must always be viewed as greater for his dignity and their love to survive.

A WOMAN IS

A MOON THAT

ORBITS A

MAN'S WORLD

The

wall

is

built

with

rationality

Nobody starts further down the mountain
than a man in sexual selection. A woman starts
on the top and slides down with age whereas a
man must understand how to make his way up.
This struggle in sexual selection is rocket fuel for
a man's rationality. He must understand his path
in order to improve his journey. That is the
reason I am writing this book. To be a guide for
men up the mountain. Too many men lack the
natural guide, a father. That is why I break down
the rationale for masculine frame. Because my
soul aches for men who have been left behind.
Men must know that behind the stone mask of
masculinity is a rationale otherwise the mask is
worn with mindless posturing. This posturing
without rationale leads to chaos and dysfunction.
Many simple men know frame because they
know that if they act like stone, it pleases a
woman. They do not need to know why; they just

know it works. Without any further knowledge of frame, they open themselves up to exploitation and might interpret a woman's behavior in a harsher way than necessary. Knowledge of sexual difference is the most important knowledge on the planet to men because men are at the mercy of a woman's innate knowledge. A woman doesn't need to read a book on how to be a woman because it is an innate experience for her. Her sexual selection is based on who she wants to surrender to. But with a man, he must learn how to pick up masculine frame to help him get up the mountain of sexual selection. Women are privileged in sexual selection early on and it makes their minds soft. They are at the mercy of age and beauty which fades with time while men must create their own sexual value through worldly success.

Rationality is a man's best friend. It is the helping voice behind the wall. It helps a man figure out his suffering and how he can improve on it. That is why increasing rationality is important to a man's masculinity. One way a man can do this is by reading and writing. Reading is the input and writing helps a man formulate his thoughts. Without formulation, thoughts exist without order. A man doesn't need to write books, but what he needs to do is keep a journal. Write down why you think what you think. The process of why, why, why builds a man's rational mind. Ask yourself "why do I do what I do?" This allows the mind to increase rationality which helps a man have a god-level view of himself. This eye above can help guide a man on his journey of masculinity. For example, in hunting a man will realize that the steps he takes breaks twigs and therefore scares game. He might look above and imagine himself sitting in a tree waiting for the game to come underneath him. This was all before he climbed the tree. Man's ability to rationalize and problem solve is at the core of our sexual selection burden. A man starts at the bottom because men are needed in the world to problem solve. By solving the problem of their sexual selection, we all get the fruits of their labor. *Men need to start at the bottom of the mountain of our sexual selection to be strong enough to be the leaders at the top.* This ability to rationalize our own existence coupled with the discipline to carry out our vision is what makes man an extraordinary beast. Read classic literature and write in your journal, not because you want to but because your masculinity needs it.

This doesn't have to be strictly literary. It can also be improved with taking things apart and putting them back together. This increases rationality as well. Take time in learning how things work and how to fix things. Increasing knowledge of mechanisms increases a man's capacity for rational thought. That is why women crave a "handy man," not just because they need things fixed but they want a rational mind around to help them emotionally. If a man lets his emotions rule him then he abandons his rational mind. To be rational is to be separate from emotional thoughts. To rise above the emotional earthly state into the heavens of logical reasoning. If a man has problems with logic, then he has problems with masculinity. Because that is what is expected of a man's leadership, not a bleeding heart but a razor-sharp mind. Leave feelings to the woman, she does them better anyhow. We must exist in the rational plane in order to guide them from the chaos they exist in.

Another way a man can increase rationality is by organization. If a man leaves his living area a mess and doesn't apply order to his body and mind then he allows irrationality to rule him. Women already have enough chaos in their lives and that is why they seek a masculine man's order. By being disciplined and orderly, a man increases the strength of his frame of reality. Rationality and order are the mortar that holds the bricks of a man's wall of masculinity together. Without order there is disbelief and where there is disbelief, there is decay. A man shouldn't doubt himself. By keeping an orderly mind and body he tells himself that he does believe. External to internal technique. This further strengthens his frame and allows him the emotional and impulse control needed for benign leadership. Hopefully, this book helps men increase their rationale and to understand the mechanics of frame. Because once a man knows why he does what he does and why other men do what they do then he is already a step ahead of a woman.

The

wall

reads

and

writes

I will continue the point of reading and
writing because of its dire need for men in our
world where women are more educated. It is
necessary now more than ever for a man to pick
up a book. Society should encourage men to be
educated and not overly encourage women. To
encourage females to be more educated than
males is a horrible design that negatively effects
our sexual selection. (Education plus the money
it provides.) Why? Because feminine intelligence
is like the snake in the original garden, it breeds
chaos in that it undermines a man's authority
within his romantic relationship.

"But Jerr," a voice calls out form outside
the page, "Is it necessary for a man to be smarter
than his woman or can masculine frame solve
this?"

Frame goes a long way in asserting
dominance over a woman, but intelligence can
flip frames. This psychology can be seen between
the interactions of raging bull types and paralyzed
deer types. "Illiterate bruisers" often dominate

"literate pansies" not just because they make easy targets but because they are a threat to their self-appointed authority. People attack based on fear. It is fear that makes a bad boy type assault a nerd type in high school. The bruiser fears being intellectually humiliated and so he goes on the offensive to physically humiliate the weakling to further secure his sexual selection options. While looks and muscles go a long way in sexual selection, if a man is made to look like a moron, then a woman will doubt his capacity for leadership. And leadership is what she craves.

"But Jerr," a voice calls out from outside the page, "ME DUMB. WHAT ME DO?"

Read and read some more. A man should always have a book on his nightstand. And don't just read non-fiction or dry history because you falsely think it's more macho to do so. Pick all kinds of books including classic literature that dives deep into human consciousness. We have a glut of vast knowledge and wisdom at our fingertips but an equal glut of laziness in reaching for it. Read Orwell, Huxley, Steinbeck and Dostoyevsky. Dig deep into the minds of these brilliant men. To read a book is to humbly submit to a writer's narration. It would be much more valuable for a man's spirit if he chose to spend time with a genius instead of brain numbing bar flies.

To understand another person's writing is to understand another person's mind. And literature and books are how we as a species share our minds with each other. Soak up as much as you can of these minds and increase intelligence for the good of your romantic relationship.

But reading is not enough for increasing intelligence, a man must also write. To read is to understand the mental framework of others while writing is how we understand our own mental framework. Writing helps a man organize and articulate his thoughts with trained clarity. When a man keeps a journal, he should not just take notes mindlessly like he is keeping inventory to a general store but rather he should form his thoughts on important matters and express them through writing. Think about something that is puzzling and try to write out solutions. That is how we train the mind for clear thinking and rationalization. The more a man reads and writes the stronger his capacity for a rational mind will be. This is especially needed for the raging bull type men who lack rationality and have impulse control issues. Reading and writing will train them to think before action which will solve a lot of their self-made drama. To read a book is an act of discipline and humility.

Plan on writing everyday not just about what happened in boring detail but rather what you thought about what happened. This is not because you want to keep a diary of your feelings like a woman but that you are exercising your rationality like a man.

PICK UP

FRAME AND

PREVENT

FEMININE

CHAOS

The

wall

controls

anger

Growing up I was surrounded by angry men. This one emotion was allowed and deemed "masculine" These angry men would lose control and threaten violence on others around them. They would fail shit tests and immediately take out their wrath on those that disrespected them. These men would turn beet red in humiliation when they failed shit tests. If people didn't respect them, they would force them to. They would react to others with high emotion and scream like a child with a temper tantrum when they didn't get their way. Does all that sound masculine? Doesn't that all sound childish and feminine in nature? The biggest hurdle many men need to get over in their head is the fetishization of their anger. They hold onto anger like security blankets that keep them safe from the reality of their real emotion. They refuse to face what they fear in their life and psyche. And so, they surrender to wrath to fool themselves into feeling in control over the uneasy feelings that twist inside them. From this weak state, they fetishize their anger in pride to showcase false control. It is not a badge of honor as some men deem it. It is shameful, weak and proof of a man who has emotional issues. If a young boy in a grocery store wants candy that a parent refuses to buy him and proceeds to throw a temper tantrum is that viewed as strength? It is entitlement, arrogance and lack of discipline. When a man punches a wall in front of a woman or child what he is saying is "This could be your head if you don't obey me." That is tyrannous leadership and a projection of fear of loss of control. If respect is forced, then respect will be resented. The first thing men need to do if they have anger problems is to call it for what is, weak and feminine.

"But Jerr," a voice calls out from off the page, "What if my woman won't obey me and she has deeply humiliated me?"

Loss of temper is a humiliation of self. Becoming angry just adds to a man's humiliation and further inspires doubt of his leadership in the woman. It doesn't solve a thing and only further digs the hole of his problem. If a woman won't obey then she is telling you that she doesn't want to be in a relationship. If she constantly humiliates you, she is telling you that she doesn't want you as her leader. The only way a man can solve these problems is by leaving the woman. If she wants to redeem herself, then the man must let her be the one to reach out. That allows her to come back under his frame with dignity.

"But Jerr," a voice calls out from off the page, "I control my anger; I just funnel it through martial arts and weight-lifting."

That is only prolonging the issue. If a man said "I am sad all the time but I'm going to use my sadness for something" that would be absurd. A framed man must overcome all the twisted feelings inside himself. By quieting down the negative emotions until they are muted is how a man exists in a rational mind. LET GO OF ANGER for your own good. Let it go and exist in a new reality where you are free of the sourness it brings. There is a whole lot that has happened to me in my life that should make me twisted but that would only cause more damage if I allowed it. When someone traumatizes us, it is an initial shock but if a man lets himself continue with aftershocks, then the trauma will stay in his body. Do not view the perpetrators of your abuse as "evil" or "wicked" but rather see them as "selfish", "callous" and "tyrannous."

When I was seven and my stepdad was throwing chairs at walls could be perpetually seen as cruel, but in retrospect with rationality, I can see that he was in fear of losing control over his own dignity. That allows me a god-level view of him and not an angry-man view of him. It allows us to control our bitterness when we clean the moral slates of others with rationality. When a man is an adult, he can set boundaries of his own dignity which protects his own belief in self. Understand that people are "evil" not because they are "demonic," but because they lack control and are callous. I've lacked control and have been callous in my own life and I don't view myself as evil. But I have learned lessons about my nature and continue to improve upon myself by being a "new person."

If people in your life have done you wrong and they continue doing you wrong, then by all means cut them out of your life to preserve your own dignity. A man does not need to forgive daily or even weekly. If a man hasn't seen a family member that has temper issues in a year just maybe that person has had a realization over their behavior. That is where forgiveness can blossom. And sometimes checking in on people on rare occasion to see if they have changed can be a positive.

I don't want to view people as unredeemable because I do not want to view myself as unredeemable and don't want others to view me as unredeemable. I do believe that people can change and become better in how they treat others. First, they must start by loving themselves. Because the biggest assholes on the planet tend to be people who hate themselves and want to spread it around. A man must stand up for his own respect and cast those people away until they learn that bad behavior sours and destroys relationships.

Anger is a reaction, not an action. When a man feels slighted by people and the world, his heart becomes bitter in anger. That is like receiving humiliation and then internally whipping your organs with stress afterwards. Be free from anger by realizing that any anger in the body is too much anger.

"But Jerr," a voice calls out a bit angry, "What about righteous anger isn't that okay? I mean there is a lot in the world that a man should be angry about..."

There is an *occasion* for righteous anger but most times righteous anger is used to justify feelings of anger inside an already-angry-guy. Angry guys speak of righteous anger only because they do not want to change their angry personality. Also "righteous anger" can mean anything, it could mean whatever a man believes it to be. The best course of action is to cast anger out of the heart and to become cold in rationality because if an execution needs to happen, we do not need an emotionally angry executioner to issue out the justice.

When men are angry, they have reactionary frames, and this state leads to many relationship issues. For example, when a woman shit tests a man with disrespect and he hollers at her, this loss of control signals to the woman weakness. What does a woman do when a man signals weakness? She reacts in offense. Why? Because her innate survival is dependent on a man leading her with rationality. If the man fails in rational leadership, then he could get not only them both killed but their offspring as well. Think about it like this. A ship captain starts to lose confidence and begins to act erratically. Who should challenge him? The first mate. It is the first mate's duty to protect the crew from a captain who has lost his mind. The same is true of a woman but it is all hidden in her ancestral memory. When a man reacts in anger by losing his temper, he shows his woman that his leadership has become erratic. This inspires a high level of fear and doubt in her heart towards him.

"But Jerr," a desperate voice calls out, "These bitches be crazy, what is a man to do?"

The only way to calm a bitch is through masculine frame. If a bitch is acting up then a man needs to firmly correct her with his words and/or remove his presence. A woman only learns through calm assertive direction and fear of loss. If a man reacts in anger, he only makes his problem worse. Also, if the bitch is in fact crazy, then a man should let her find love inside the asylum.

When a man loses his temper, he allows his frame to react to his woman's frame and she will react as women do, with more energy. If the guy keeps it going, they will both keep bouncing frames back and forth in reaction like two lesbians playing frame tennis.

Don't react to her. Don't lose your head and do not lose your cool. It is the coolness of the wall that attracts a woman's touch. She likes the cold masculine nature because it cools her down. If a man is hot headed, he only inflames a woman's feminine nature. These hot head type guys increase the bad nature in their women by their own feminine frame.

It starts with the man to turn away and to keep frame. He doesn't let a woman shit test him into abandoning his wall. He stays behind the wall eternal. Remember, that is the shit test "Will this guy leap out from his wall in weakness or will he keep frame." That is the test that she wants to know. If a man stays behind his wall he succeeds, and this reassures the woman of his stable masculinity. Women are emotionally unstable by nature and they will always believe their way is the best way. In her head she thinks "I'm emotional because I am right and if I get him emotional, then that will prove that he agrees with me." But when a man gets emotional this only inflames a woman's anxiety (because a woman should never get what she wants) and sinks their argument further. If a man displays a cool rational head this calms the woman's chaotic nature under his frame which she'll appreciate later after the fight is over.

How does a man conquer his anger? The best way for a man to remove something from his mind is to view such thing as weak and feminine. *Anger and wrath are weaknesses.* It does nothing positive and only sours a man's insides. It should be perceived as gross and bile. When a man loses his temper, it is as if he vomits out all his childish emotions to everyone in his vicinity. Do not hold the anger inside but rather cast it out completely from your body. Get your mind off what makes you angry and start filling your mind with whatever frees you from anger. That is the start. When something triggers your temper view it as frame practice by controlling it. If a man has temper issues this could be a way to desensitize himself by controlled therapy. Maybe start by controlling cursing when you stub your toe. Something small like that can help a man control how he reacts under pain and duress. Keep the wall cool to the touch.

The

wall

does

not

budge

A woman's mind is like the ever-changing wind. When she has made up her mind about something, she will be the first one to talk herself out of it. This indecisiveness is feminine in nature. Every month her hormones control her, and this biological instability has a major effect on her decision process. Up down, yes, no and maybe. That is why women reward the certainty of walls with sex and respect. A woman innately craves the certitude of a man's mind. He is the rock that comforts her during emotional chaos. If a man lacks certainty, then his mind will be indecisive. Perpetually lacking certitude is not humility, it is disbelief of self. A man might not know which way in the fork road to walk but he still decides anyhow. He doesn't become paralyzed before his options. If a man's indecisiveness paralyzes him because of the weight of options before him, then he lacks what it takes to lead. *Because leaders must make decisions and project certainty without one hundred percent certainty.* Being immediate in choosing the lesser of two evils is a leadership skill and women crave this in a man.

Many men lack the power of belief within themselves to pick one option over the next. Inside their minds they hear a voice full of doubt saying "Who are you to decide, do you even know? If you said you know isn't that a lie?" And so on and so on. Unframed men who based their personality on "just be yourself" think that it is better to be openly doubtful and true than to give the appearance of false confidence. They do not get that *leadership is truth*. That the capacity of making a quick-draw decision is what is required of leadership because in some scenarios option-paralysis means a mind has become lost and confused. In times past when women were more dependent on men for survival, they depended on a man to make hard calls for them both. The weight and responsibility of direction fell on the shoulders of the man. If he couldn't decide, then it was up to the woman and she had to bear his load for him. That is why women innately require a man with a leader's mind. When a man expresses uncertainty, he inspires fright within his woman and children. They need a man to bear the burden of anxiety hidden from view from them and for him to overcome his own anxiety to lead them to success.

A woman will shit test a man with her own uncertainty. For example, it can be as simple as dinner plans. If man decides on the restaurant to eat at and the woman offers up a different choice, this is a shit test. She wants the man to be ruled with uncertainty like she is.

"But Jerr," a hungry voice calls out from outside the page, "What if she just doesn't want to eat at the burrito place again and wants to try something new?"

If a man agrees to the woman's choice, then a common occurrence is the woman will again change her mind. She increases the testing because the man already gave in once. The man said Mexican, the woman offered Chinese and then added a wildcard of Greek at the ending. If the man says "Okay instead of the burrito place I want, or the Chinese place you just said you wanted, we will go to the Greek place you finally suggested."

As soon as he is done figuring out what he wants on the Greek menu the woman will go back to a previous choice. "Maybe burritos DO sound good..." she will muse to herself going full circle back to the man's initial choice. She shifted her shit test from second to third gear then grinded back to first. The feminine indecisiveness engines are beginning to roar.

"But Jerr," a voice calls out from off the page, "What is a man to do? Should he punch a wall, scream at her or just eat at home?"

First off, a man should just choose where to eat. If the woman offers a suggestion, then just tell her that you both can eat at that place next time. If a man allows himself to be carried away with feminine indecision from Mexican to Chinese to Greek and back to Mexican, he should nail it shut at the last choice the woman made. "We're eating Greek."

In the future he should bear the responsibility of dinner decisions himself.

For a man to become framed he must conquer his own self-doubt and hide it behind his wall from his woman. He should work on gaining a reputation of certitude. *Better to be seen as arrogant than to be seen as lacking confidence within romance.* A woman's ancestral memory prefers arrogance to uncertainty. Because making a bad decision is better than being caught up with fear while wolves are at your back. That is why it is important to reassure a woman of masculine certitude. She needs to believe that you believe in yourself otherwise she will become filled with anxiety. Uncertainty is chick repellent.

The wall is calm and certain. That is one reason why shit tests exist. It is a way for a woman to test how truly calm and how truly certain a man is. The more a man passes these tests the more reassured the woman becomes in his leadership. Practice immediacy in deciding choices and do not budge when a decision has been made. Keep your wall certain.

The

wall

should

intimidate

The same element that keeps a man from being picked on by other men is the same quality that women are sexually attracted to. The "don't mess with me look." This doesn't mean a man needs to look like a violent criminal but rather that his physical presence projects strength. The mere look alone of a man can attract fights or prevent them. It has to do with how heavy his presence looks to people around him. How much fear exists in his eyes and how proud does he carry his posture? How much muscle weight does he have on him and how tall is he? (Short guys need to amplify other areas from the lack.) A man shouldn't try to look like a criminal because that would mean that is how he wants the world to view him, but he shouldn't look like a dandy either.

Masculine frame is both internal and external. A man's physical body can look feminine just like a woman's body can look masculine. The physical opposite of gender type is what women crave. To feel feminine, a woman wants to feel small-and-vulnerable. If a woman is big and the man is overly skinny this makes the woman self-conscious of her masculine presence which kicks her farther away from the vulnerable state of feminine orgasm. She wants to be dominated by a larger and stronger man. She wants a protector not a protectee. Lift heavy weights that boost testosterone. Don't be too skinny or too fat. Both attract negative attention and women don't want the anxiety of being next to what draws heat. Think about that. A woman is an anxious and self-aware creature that feels heightened anxiety when negative attention is cast upon her. If she stands next to a man who looks like he is going to get his lunch money stolen, then she too will feel like her lunch money is going to get stolen and that she might have to protect her man. A woman becomes full of anxiety and dread when she must assume the protector role over a man.

A man who makes an effort to lift weights is a man who takes his masculine role as protector seriously. It doesn't take that much muscle to attract a woman or to project a "don't mess with me" appearance. It just takes a little training, and most guys shrug even that small responsibility.

If a guy is half a woman's weight with a nerd neck, then he will not project enough backbone to stave off intruders. The necessary amount of intimidation isn't just purely physical but mental as well. How a man looks in his eye says more about his backbone than his bicep. If a man darts his eyes around nervously and cannot sustain eye-contact are both indicators that he is cowardly with a nervous nature. This man fears violence more than he desires respect. To be a man is to be ready to fight. If a man's dignity is on the line, he should try his best to walk away from a confrontation with his dignity intact (charisma), but he shouldn't just allow others to piss freely on his wall without recompense. To stand up for dignity is to be ready for violence. There is a line in Shakespeare's Julius Caesar, "A coward dies a thousand times before his death but the valiant taste of death but once." This quote has had a big impact of how I view the threat of violence in my own spirit. The violence I was surrounded by as a child paralyzed me in fear and created a cowardly spirit. The older I became the more each act of cowardice felt like a death of my spirit, as if the humiliation alone was as painful as a real dagger into my heart. Cowardice is real trauma to dignity and dignity is what makes life worth living. After being bullied and humiliated enough, a punch to the face would illicit less pain than the lasting pain to the spirit by shrinking in fear.

The best help for a cowardly spirit is to be exposed to the object of fear. This allows the body and mind to become desensitized to the fear response while proving that the fantasy of fear was nothing more than cowardly illusion.

Making simple changes like looking men in the eye when walking past them in hallways at work is a step into the right direction. Make them be the first to break frame with a nod or smile. Just stare at them dead center in the eye and wait for it. If they ask you what's wrong just keep walking and they will often ignore. When I practiced this, I called it "stealing souls" when the man turned away first. Make it a game. After a while, the body will be ready for conflict instead of being stuck in flight mode.

This only applies to more neurotic men and not to hot head types since they have the opposite issue. A hot head type guy needs less reasons for confrontation and additional help on how to apply charisma to protect dignity. For example, if a nervous guy and a hot head were both walking though the hallway at work and the nervous guy attempts to "steal the soul" of the hot head guy, the first thing this would do to the hot head is compel him to say, "What the fuck are you looking at?" But since he is working on himself too, he could just nod his head at the nervous guy.

For the hot head, this untrains his confrontational and heated nature into the calm demeanor needed for rational leadership. If the nervous guy keeps going down the hall without responding to the hot head, the angry guy gets another lesson to work on. Instead of saying "That fucking stupid ass bitch" in his heart he could say "What's wrong with that guy? Is he practicing stealing souls for his masculinity?" He just needs to flip the script of his programming.

For men, battling fear it to chase what keeps them paralyzed. Every act of bravery is rocket fuel for a man's masculine frame. Why? Because standing up for what you believe in further solidifies that belief. And what is more important than a man's belief in his own dignity? Seek out every shadow of fear and shine a brave light on it.

149

Emotions

weaken

the

wall

The reason a man breaks his frame is because he becomes overwhelmed by emotion and the emotions bleed out by way of expression. The biggest problem with modern day man is he has bought into the lie of "just be yourself" and been told that "big boys don't cry" is toxic masculinity. And that all relationship problems can be settled through verbal communication. This personal philosophy of expression-is-good-and-healthy is what robs many men of the internal fortitude needed to carry a masculine frame. They cannot keep up a walled presence for long because they lack emotional control and depend on validation. If a man is attempting the wall of masculinity, he must learn to control the spirits within. If a sentimental song or movie makes a man cry, this signals to the woman that the wall is hiding lies. It shows her that the man's strength is for show and that the bricks on his wall are merely wallpaper to deceive women into believing he is strong. When this happens to a man, he should expect to see more shit tests after breaking frame. The woman is going to want to test him out further to be sure of the soundness of his posturing like peeling wallpaper to reveal the wall behind. She doesn't want to put all her trust in something that will come tumbling down with a little pressure. That is why a man must train himself in emotional control.

"But Jerr," a voice calls out form off the page, "How do we control emotions... Don't we just have emotions?"

If fear can diminish within the body, then so can anxiety and sadness. How do we conquer fear? We expose ourselves to what makes us afraid while not shrinking back. This creates internal strength and builds fortitude. Without training, a man will be controlled by any emotion he has just as he is controlled by fear. *Desensitization therapy is the key to calming what stirs.* The Guatemalan special forces known as Kaibiles would have their recruits raise and bond with a puppy before being ordered to kill it. This would traumatize the soldier into a calloused state. Sound horrific? I agree but it still had a powerful effect on their frames. Don't worry, I will not suggest killing puppies to help with your masculinity. But the psychology of the training shows that we must be able to kill what we love. Each man must figuratively kill his attachments based on sentimentality. When men are brought up by dominant women, they end up loving their emotional selves. Why? Because they were told to "just be yourself" and that expression is positive. So how can emotions and the expression of them be bad? And how can a personality based on being emotional be bad? Wouldn't that make our true self bad?

That is what a man must kill. He must kill his own emotional personality. He must kill what he loves. When a man first picks up masculine frame he will feel like he is killing his personality because all his awesome thoughts will have no release and his awesomeness cannot be explained in detail to his woman. Will she miss this beautiful original being? No, a woman will not miss it, in fact she will reward the lack of personality with sex and respect. She knows how difficult it is to hide the emotional spirit. That is what a woman respects, bodily control. Women do not respect women because women do not respect unrestrained expression of ego. They want a man to hold back his personality so that a mystery can form inside themselves. This masculine discipline is appreciated by women because they are overwhelmed with emotions. They feel weak to hold back themselves from their own expression and see masculine discipline as foreign. That is why opposites attract.

When I was unframed my anxiety was high, and I sincerely believed that a woman would appreciate every word that came out of my mouth. And thought that unless a man presented a unique personality to a woman there would be nothing for her to attach herself to. When women showed attention to framed men, I would think that the women were confused. Why would they reward such boring men when I was being more expressive and showing them more personality? Do you see how confused and arrogant I was?

A man's personality doesn't exist on his tongue, it exists in his woman's head. It cannot be force fed. When a man picks up frame which diminishes his public persona many people will reject his posturing and mourn the loss of the "real guy." Why? Because people love what they know and they feel for weakness. It is easier to love a giggly baby than a silent biker. But who gets more respect? The formula is: expression gets love, but suppression gets respect. When a man changes by picking up masculine frame not only is he killing what he loved but he is killing what others loved. And good riddance! A man shouldn't care about love when he is being humiliated and disrespected. Leave love to women and children. Men must be respected because we all innately have masculine pride. A man's love life is more important than his aunt wondering what happened to the personality of her nephew. Let them mourn the loss of that weak self and never look back. Think about it like this, if a man who used to be hunched over and used to be mocked for being a hunchback but later corrected his posture and right after his friends said, "Where is the ol' Hunchy that we love?" wouldn't this boil the man's blood? They miss the familiarity even if it brought more suffering into a man's life. Most times it is the ones that profess to love us that are the ones that fear a positive change within us. A man should just pursue the path of his greatest dignity and let those that don't understand continue not understanding. They are not living his life and they will not tell him to pursue respect over love. A man must create his own backbone and build his own desire for respect. That is the most important goal of being a framed man. A man avoids the trauma of humiliation by setting an expectation that he prefers respect over affection. The wall is the precedent for change. It says "Here I am, a man wanting respect. I am no longer the jester you knew; I am a king." At first people will laugh and mock you but after a while they will adjust their expectations. If they do not, then a man should confront them and address their disrespect. To be a king a man must correct those that assume him a jester. If they still do not want to respect then they must be abandoned. A man should not continue association with those that truly do not care about his overall wellbeing.

Some people in a man's life will reject the new him because he is now posing a threat to the respect that they are used to receiving. They think, "I liked him weak because treating him as a jester made me feel more like a king." That is the sickness within them. These people are not truly friends but exploiters.

"But Jerr," a voice calls out from off the page, "How do I control emotions? I get emotional frequently."

To control emotions, a man must practice control his own behaviorism. When a man wants to say something but doesn't, this helps him with speech control. The same can be done with emotional control. Remember, the external to internal technique. One way a man can practice is by inciting emotion and controlling his reaction to that incitation. This can be done by watching a sad movie and holding back tears. This can be done by watching a funny movie and not laughing. These are frame control practices. Every time a man successfully controls an expression of an emotion, it further quiets the emotions within him. *Exterior control is interior control.* With more control on the outside, the emotions will settle down within. If a man expends his energy through exercise and avoids junk foods that create low energy, he will further help himself with emotional control.

"But Jerr," a voice calls out from off the page, "What if a man feels a tear forming in the back of his eye and he knows he is about to cry in front of his woman. What should he do?"

Flee the room. Make up an excuse and go cry to yourself alone. That is the masculine way. And after you have a cry, admit to yourself that it was a failure of masculinity. It may feel like a relief after the tears come out, but it truly is a humiliation to masculine spirit of emotional discipline. Look yourself in the mirror and tell yourself to be strong. Never tell yourself that you are worthless or weak. NEVER fuel your own disbelief.

Ponder on what crying represents. When a man cries, he is signaling to the world that he cannot handle his emotional reality. "This reality is too much to bear, here come the waterworks." That is what happens when a man thinks something is too hard or too terrible to imagine. A framed man can imagine hell itself and not shrink back. Surgeons must cut into bodies to save them. Hunters must kill animals to feed families. Men must kill intruders to protect their families. All these things are horrific to the spirit but men bear the burden of reality for women so they can remain in their feminine spirit. That is why it is important to project strength of emotional control to her. So, she can exist in the emotional feminine without worrying about the horror of being alive.

The good thing about living behind a wall is it gets easier. If a guy is just picking up frame and feels overwhelmed, just remember every day you carry frame is a day of not being disrespected like your previous self. Never go back to the old personality. The old personality is dead and gone. Long live respect and the wall that receives it.

The

wall

does

not

seek

validation

Emotions lead to chaos. The more a man lacks control over his emotions and lacks control over impulse, the more his life will fill with the chaos it draws. Bad decisions breed bad results, and nothing creates more bad decisions than a man following his emotions. That is why when women become unbounded in society their lives become full of regret and suffering. We currently live in a time where there is a concerted effort to avoid shame labels for a woman's promiscuous nature and avoid shame labels for a woman's obesity. Both represent unrestrained chaos. The body increases in decay if not exercised and properly nourished just as a promiscuous woman's mental health will rapidly decay with the accumulated psychological damage she received from her casual sexual encounters.

The dominant feminine view is to lean towards permissiveness. This goes along with the feminine framework of making an environment weaker (or just seem weaker) to accommodate a weak self. "Instead of me losing weight, I will change the whole world to say that obesity it is in fact healthy and that all men will just tell me I'm beautiful regardless of my looks."

A woman's nature is to emotionally control others through gaslighting. This gaslighting approach is how dominant women rule their home with guilt and shame tactics. When I was growing up with my single mom, she would incite me to confess. "What is the matter?", "I know something is wrong", "You would feel better if you just let me know what is going on inside." This approach is to micro-manage emotions (feminine) with constant attention. A single mother is overwhelmed by reality herself and if she is trying to be a good mom, she will try to raise good boys. This creates an unhealthy relationship between mother and child which weakens a boy's internal frame of reality. He becomes dependent on his mother's validation for his own feeling of purity to cleanse his conscience. Many men are brought up in a confessor-state because they were ruled under a woman's dominant frame. The woman is not trying to be evil, she is doing the only thing she knows, talking and emotional validation. Once a boy is emotionally dependent on his mother, she can control his mind with relative ease. By controlling his emotional state, she can make sure he does what she wants. When a mother does this, she wants her boy to be virtuous and not a criminal. It comes from a good place in her heart. She is not trying to create a puppet for illicit reasons, but she still wants to create a puppet for perceived greater morality of the boy.

When men are in relationships and they were raised this way, they will be confessors to their women. This creates a shift in the power dynamic and places authority on the woman's shoulders. The unstable frame in the man creates anxiety in his woman because it projects that he needs her for emotional support and validation of his morality. When a woman must emotionally support a man, she will resent him for being weak. Why? Because a woman needs a man for emotional support. She is consumed with anxiety and doubt about her own emotional state. She wants a man that can not only bear his own internal reality but can help her with her internal state as well. That is why confessor-type-guys have relationship issues. This behavior was instilled in them from a young age from a dominant mother and takes work to overcome.

Being raised by a dominant mother puts a man in a mindset primed for feminine authority. Since he was raised with a strong feminine frame over him, he will think that women should hold authority over him and that if a woman thinks he is "bad," then he must therefore be bad. This lack of belief in his own spirit creates an anxious frame of reality within him. Uncertainty of self comes about when a boy is dominated completely because his mother (or parents) lacked faith in him. This can haunt men well into old age. Hopefully, a man can break the spell long before dirt is thrown over him.

By creating a "good boy" a mother also creates a "nice guy" who places women on a holy plane in his mind. Women to him are wise sages and spirit cleansers. They can heal a man's emotional trauma. Sound rational or does it sound like a bunch of hooey? A woman only knows how to inflame trauma, she does not know how to cure it. That is why women go to talk therapy eternal. They never get cured, only billed for another week. Talking only makes things worse. Unframed men will see this when they try to go to couple's therapy or when they sit and talk about a problem in their relationship for hours. All the talk further solidifies the feminine way as the superior way and the man stays under the feminine frame of authority.

Do not confess and do not talk it out. These are not the masculine ways of handling problems in a relationship. A woman should mostly be talking to herself in her head about relationship issues. Why? Because when a man is silent, his woman becomes both his defendant and prosecutor. And if the man's frame is strong enough, the woman will plead his case best in her own imagination.

When a man talks, he enters a woman's battlefield and is not equipped to master her in that environment. Women are naturally better with communication than men. So, when a man and woman discuss problems in a relationship, the woman will have the edge in negotiation. And if a man opens his mouth, his woman's imagination is immediately killed thereby killing his greatest defense. Speak and kill imagination.

When women in our modern society use shame tactics to lessen their sexual burden is a shit test for a better deal. They know that through shame, men can be controlled. And an entire generation of men are already programmed to crumble before feminine guilt tactics which makes control easier. If a woman calls a man a sexist, he must prove he is not. If a woman calls a man "fat-phobic", then he must be a bad guy for not wanting to fuck a land whale. When society becomes feminized, shame and guilt tactics become the predominant way of control. But it only works if a man's frame of reality is dependent on a woman's validation. That is why is necessary for each man to *shatter the feminine frame of authority within his mind.* If he does so he will be free to rule himself without need to confess or to feel guilt. A man should view a woman as a silly emotional creature, not his leader of morality. To feel guilt is to feel doubt and anxiety. The guiltiest men on the planet are unframed men who have been trained to loathe their masculinity and have been trained to depend on women for moral validation.

In many relationships with a dominant woman there will be an anxious and guilty man standing behind her. He is controlled by her manipulation of his weak emotional state with shame tactics. Her tactic is for mind control.

"But Jerr," a voice calls out from off the page, "Don't women feel guilty for gaslighting men into shame?"

All is fair in love and war. If a man is weak enough to be exploited and manipulated then the woman feels like a hunter who shot a grizzly. Did the hunter feel guilt for killing the grizzly or exhilaration in the accomplishment? (I understand unframed men do not represent a grizzly, but women view all men with the standards of the highest value man. "Men" to a woman does not represent the grocery baggers but rather the CEOs.) Maybe both and that is what most women feel. They feel an accomplishment in winning against a man but also guilt in the man being so easy to beat. What is the best way for a woman to solve this problem for herself? She will flee her guilt by seeking a stronger man she does not have to feel guilty with. That is how women think in relationships with weak men. "This guy makes me feel awful about myself because he lets me abuse and exploit him. I'm going to have to escape to save my sanity."

Women escape to walls because they cannot handle how they act over a man without a wall. Weak men create cruel women. It is the man's fault for being weak and a woman knows this. When a man depends only on himself physically and emotionally, this calms a woman down under his frame. She becomes virtuous and submissive. The same woman with a weak guy would be cruel and dominant. The woman hasn't changed, only the man. A woman is merely a reflection of the man she is with. When a man picks up frame in a relationship his woman will fall into femininity. She will be grateful that she does not have to bear reality for them both.

The

wall

looks

away

When a woman respects a man, she will try to read his expressions. It is the "What is my leader thinking?" mode when a woman is in her submissive frame. She will look on her framed man's face for clues to what might be on his mind. She wants to know because she has genuine interest in unpacking his thoughts. When he gives away a clue by micro-expression this allows her to interpret him with her feminine intuition. She knows what her leader is thinking based on small clues on his face. The leader looks away and the follower looks at the leader. For example, if an unframed man is watching a comedy with his woman, he most likely will be laughing more and looking over at his woman to see if she is agreeing with his sense of humor. *He looks to her for validation of himself.* When a framed man is watching a comedy, he will allow his woman to break frame first which propels her to look at his face for validation of her sense of humor. The wall looks away and the woman looks to the wall for reassurance. This can be said of many different scenarios where the woman, as a follower, looks to her man as leader for validation about reality. The psychology of a man looking away is that he should be more concerned with the environment than his woman. The ancestral reasoning is that a woman will be busy looking after children while her man is busy looking out for them all. If a man has his eyes constantly on his woman, then he is not watching out for danger like a protector should.

This programming applies to something as silly as watching a movie. (Our bodies follow the same ancestral algorithm regardless of triviality of circumstance.) A man shouldn't care if his woman likes the same things he likes, he should just concern himself with his own wants and desires while letting the woman have greater expression in viewing his likes. If a man likes a movie, all he needs to do is watch the movie a couple times which will let her know how much she likes the movie. If a man likes a song all he needs to do is listen to the song a few times and the woman will know he likes the song. Unframed men narrate their own pleasure. If an unframed man likes a movie, he will tell the woman "This movie is good" or if he likes a song, he will let the woman know "I like this song." This is all cornball behavior and robs a woman of liking her man's likes based on her own intuition. Unframed men narrate everything because they doubt feminine intuition. By doubting intuition an unframed man is in effect doubting femininity. He would rather just tell a woman what to like instead inspiring her to like what he likes. *Unframed men are tyrannous by nature and force their wants without inspiring desire.* That is the magic that a framed man provides for a woman. He trusts her imagination and intuition to align herself with him. If she doesn't align herself, then she is telling him that she has low interest in him.

When a man looks away from a woman, it signals to her his independence of thought and will. It projects to a woman that a man has a mind of his own and doesn't require her for validation of his own existence. Why? Because when a man can afford to look away from an object of desire means he has wealth of self-belief. Unframed men are in constant disbelief of themselves and that state of belief-poverty increases the anxiety within their women.

How a man uses his eyes is a display of human understanding. There is a Benjamin Franklin quote (his intelligence was off the charts, unfortunately so was his hedonism) "When you speak to a man, look on his eyes; When he speaks to thee, look on his mouth."

Like most Benjamin Franklin's thoughts this one is a beauty. Why look at man's eyes when speaking and his mouth when he is speaking? One reason would be that when a person is speaking to you, they want to search for your eyes without the heavy spotlight o attention making them feel self-conscious. Looking deep into someone's eyes when they speak will project neediness and inflate their ego beyond their own belief. In their head they are wondering, "I am not saying anything particularly interesting and my thoughts are not that special, so this person must be desperate and a fool to give me so much attention."

Eye contact has its own currency and a man willing to give everyone equal eye contact does not value his own eyes.

Why look at someone's eyes when speaking to them? Because they want to see the truth and authority in your eyes when you speak. It has been said the eyes are the windows into the soul. Why? Because by looking into another person's eyes we gauge their truth. Shifty eyes signal falsehood and unhealthy-looking eyes signal a debauched lifestyle. The eyes signal self-confidence in belief of self. Unframed men will feel anxiety with eye contact because they lack self-belief in their authority. That is why they will cast their eyes to the wall in anxiety. When a woman sees a man giving her too much eye-contact this signals that he needs too much validation of his self. When he cannot look her in the eyes when he speaks is a giveaway that he lacks confidence of self. Master the eyes and do not let them give away your weakness.

Unframed men use their entire face for expression whereas a framed man uses mostly his upper portion of face for expression. From above he allows his eyes and eyebrows to subtly give away his thought process. This attracts attention to his eyes which builds further interest in his authority of speech. *Eyes are more trusted than lips.* When a framed man uses his eyes for soft communication, he allows his audience to focus on the most trusted part of the face.

The walled experience is a looking forward existence. A man behind the wall of masculinity will master the peripheral view of the world. From the corner of his eye, he will see his woman's glances and she will peer into his eyes with interest. She is trying to read him, and he knows it. That is the dynamic of a king and his woman. (I did not say queen because I did not want to vomit.) When a man looks away from his woman, he gives her an opportunity to do what women do best, decipher micro expressions. An unframed man who narrates his every little thought and makes sure to over express lest his woman does not understand, is a thief of her intuition. He robs her of imagination and autonomy of interpretation. A woman with an unframed man feels like he is in the spotlight and she is non-existent. Everything is about him. This builds resentment in her and she will start planning her trip to a nearby wall. Why? Because she wants to be with a man who allows her to be a woman. Life is short and if a woman is with an unframed man, she is losing years of femininity and all the arousing pleasures that come with it. It is not good enough to simply be alive, each individual man and woman must get what they most desire. For a man, it is respect and sex. For a woman, it is a man's masculine frame and the femininity that it inspires in her. A woman will not just "be a woman" or just "be feminine" or just "be submissive," she must have a frame that inspires those things in her. When unframed men have relationship issues, they will just demand women be those things without inspiring them to be those things. The wall inspires submission. That is why a woman will glance over at a man after she laughs and does not hear a laugh from him. From his side eye he will see her longingly search for meaning from his walled presence. The wall looks away and the woman looks to the wall.

ABANDON THE

WEAK SELF THAT

WAS CREATED

FROM THE

INEXPERIENCE OF

YOUTH

The

wall

seeks

its

own

pleasure

    In my unframed past I remember thinking to myself about the selfishness of masculine frame and thinking framed men were "jerks" in their relationships. They seemed greedy for power with their posturing. They seemed like they placed their own pleasure above the pleasure of their women. Looking back, I can see how confused I was while being partially correct. A framed man does place his own pleasure above his woman's, but this simultaneously gives pleasure to the woman. Framed men know that by worrying about a woman's pleasure is the easiest way to rob a woman of pleasure. They know that a woman expects a degree of selfishness from her leader. The wall is selfish, and the woman rewards the masculine selfishness by riding-in-the-wake of a man's pleasure. The man focuses on himself and this allows the woman to surrender herself into his frame-of-arousal. When a man worries about his woman's pleasure above his own is a sign of fear and projects weakness. How can a woman experience her feminine pleasure when she is being bombarded by fear projection? A man leads his own pleasure, and a woman joins or does not. That is up to her. It is a woman's role to either join her man's pleasure or not. A woman doesn't have to worry about leading her pleasure when a man leads for them both. This is not strictly about sex, otherwise I would have included this in "The wall fucks" chapter. This goes beyond sex into a man's pleasure of all things. A woman's pleasure is her man's pleasure. She will join her man in pleasure as long as he allows her to freely join it and does not demand it like an unframed man. An unframed man will fall over backwards trying to please his woman and then will build resentment when she does not share the same joy that is in his heart. That is the psychology of the unframed man. He tries to force a woman into femininity with one hand while robbing her of femininity with the other. He will give, give, give to her, and then expect it all back plus interest otherwise his feelings get hurt. These hurt feelings will turn to sourness in his spirit which will twist him into an impotent passive aggressive state. "Be nice like me or *else*" he threatens her. That is why women exploit "nice guys" because they see through the act. Women understand that a man's "niceness" is a ploy for his own pleasure. Genuine kindness comes from freely giving without expected reciprocation. When a man says "I'm a real nice guy when I get everything I want, and if I don't YOU WILL PAY" is a man in his feminine nature.

How does a "nice" guy payback his woman who will not pay him his due in respect and sex? He will pay her back in poisonous passive aggressive behaviors like a woman. He will get her back through shadow with emotional daggers. That is why women hate unframed men. Because these men are hidden with a fake smile while frowning resentment beneath.

A woman freely gives to a wall because she wants to please a man who earns respect. Note that. Earns respect. Just like everything in this world, respect is not freely given but earned. The wall itself commands respect for a man and women understand the arrangement innately. That is why they allow the wall to have the first fruits of pleasure. In a woman's ancestral memory, she knows that a man has risked his life to provide resources for her and he needs the best part of the kill. He is selfish for them all. Without him they all die. This is the programming that is deep in womankind and will not be changed by a couple generations of modern feminism. When a man puts his needs above a woman, this allows to her to be in alignment with her ancient. There is nothing nice about reality. Reality is brutal and gets harder until we are buried deep. And nobody understands the brutality of existence better than a woman. That is why she gives gifts to the wall. A woman will offer up sex and respect to a man's wall and is reassured by his selfishness because his will is needed for both of their success. He needs to have first pick of the kill for him to have what he needs for the future kill. When a wall takes what he wants, he eases the worry of his woman's mind. Be selfish for her.

The

wall

does

not

wait

One of the most common shit tests a
woman gives a man is having him wait longer
than he wants when going out to dinner. This sets
the frame of the schedule based on the woman's
time. Why does she take longer? Because she
wants to look good for him is the standard reply.
But that is false otherwise she would have started
her preparation earlier. She is purposely slowing
down the schedule on him in dominance. Ways
to get around this are to give women false
schedules for them to disobey which allows
correct timing. This is a soft shit test which
doesn't require a lot of attention in its disrespect.
But it does show us a man's mind and a woman's
mind. Women are more prone to a waiting
attitude while framed men are prone to
immediacy. That is why we have the expression
of "man of action" and not "waiting man" The
level of immediacy in a man is essential for his
masculinity. Men create inventions to save
people time. Because men know how valuable
time is to individuals. Timing is important to an
engine in a car, timing is important to a stand-up

comic when selling a joke and timing is important to a man when commanding respect.

When an unframed man gets disrespected, he will fill with indignation and he will wait. Why? Because he lacks immediacy in commanding respect. This mindset will encourage him to be passive aggressive and warped in emotion. An unframed man will sit on a bad feeling until the feeling grows in poison and consumes his spirit. These feelings curdle in him like soured milk only because he didn't pour them out sooner. It was his own fault in inaction and in waiting like a woman. Is dignity going to come knocking on a man's wall or does he have to knock for his own respect? It is crucial for a man to work on immediacy when seeking respect. One thing I've noticed is that some women will attempt to humiliate an unframed man in public. Why? Because a woman feels safe to disrespect her man by being surrounded by other people as well as signaling to members of her tribe the weakness of her man. The former comes from feeling safe to abuse while the latter comes from letting her circle know his undignified weak state to increase sympathy for herself. She is showing them based on her ancestral programming that she is with a weak man and is desperate for survival.

"But Jerr," a voice calls out from outside the page, "My woman humiliated me last night while at dinner with friends and I didn't want to make a scene, so I waited until afterwards to let her know, is that correct?"

NO. Women wait and men act. If a woman disrespects you in front of a crowd, then you stand up and let her know her disrespect right there before God and everyone. Turn the tables on her bad attitude. She should feel immense shame for disrespecting a man's masculine pride before others. Remember, a woman who disrespects her leader is deserving of little pity or sympathy. She disrespects the holiest thing on our planet, and we must protect it with quickness. Disrespect in public is a hundred times worse than disrespect in private. It must be dealt with a calm assertive approach "Why are you disrespecting me in front of others?" This simple question will shed light on her vulgar attitude and will naturally incite her to submit in apology. Many times, a woman will disrespect a man with social anxiety in front of others. Why? Because women attack a man's weak spot when they resent him. It is up to the man to defend his own honor without expecting others to. A backbone is only good if a man uses it. And he should be immediate in its use. By waiting to talk about an issue, a man is projecting to the woman that he lacks action and that he has a fear of speaking up. The talk-later-attitude is weak and ineffective. That is why when a man waits to talk later will have little impact on changing his woman's behavior for the future. Only when he learns to be quick in his command for respect will his woman learn. Why? Because to be quick to defend something is to be aware of its value. If a man loved his dog, would he allow someone to come inside his home and abuse it? Would he let them abuse it and talk to them later or will he immediately intercede? A man believes in the love he has for his dog and so he acts. The same is true with a man and his masculine pride. A man who waits to defend his honor is a man who projects to others that he does not genuinely believe in his dignity. That is why if a slight is small, a man should just ignore it for next time instead of the talk later approach. Just let it go and learn a lesson to be immediate next time. The waiting is proof of disbelief and words will not solve that. When a man is unframed, often he will not even notice disrespect (because he gets such frequent disrespect that a lot passes by unnoticed) and other times he knows he is disrespected but he lacks the balls to defend his honor quickly because he needs time to judge it. The more time a man stews on a perceived disrespect is proof that he doesn't know himself enough for immediacy. And if he doesn't know himself then how can he believe in himself? Practice taking a quick stand because you know exactly who you are.

The

wall

provides

Even in a world where women are more formally educated than men and where they can provide for themselves, they still want a man who can provide. Why? Because they are ancestrally trained. In the past a man would spend his time hunting for resource while the woman nested with their offspring. In our times a person making money is the modern-day hunt. If a man cannot make money, this signals to the woman's primordial brain that he cannot hunt. That is why a man must take his job, career and business seriously. Instead of catching game, we catch dollars. If a woman catches two dollars and a man can only catch one, then this is like her being able to catch two deer and him only one. If a woman is the more supreme hunter in the relationship, this humiliates them both. That is just one way feminism has harmed the sexual selection of our species. When a society encourages women to be providers is a societal planning blunder of massive proportions and one reason feminism must fade away in the garbage bin of bad ideas.

"But Jerr," a voice calls out from off the page, "What is a man to do in our current society where women tend to make more money?"

Work and pride your work more than her work. A man might only kill one deer compared to her two, but he must take more pride in his own kill. Pride is the answer to many relationship issues. Also, a man should always control the money in the relationship. If the woman makes more than her man then that means he has control over more. She must ask permission to spend money that she earned. The power is in the man's hands. Think about the following psychology. Who makes more money the prostitute or the pimp? Isn't it the prostitute that earns the money and then gives it all over to her pimp? (I am not condoning the violence that pimps perpetrate on prostitutes) The making of the money isn't the issue, it is who has control over the money is the core issue. A man must control the frame of money and this will calm his woman's primordial mind.

For a man to be a good provider he must take his development seriously. Every economy around the world has differences but some things never change. A man can choose a working man's profession (tangible), or he can choose a man of letters profession (abstract). Both take different skills and talents of personality which depends on whether the man enjoys more abstract thoughts or would rather work with his hands in his career. Both are needed in society and either one will provide him the dignity of knowing a skill while supplying him economic independence.

If a man is a carpenter and he is in a relationship with a woman who is a lawyer then carpentry is more essential and more deserving of pride. It doesn't matter about the money if the man makes his work seem more important than his woman's work. An attitude goes a long way in projecting dignity.

When a man takes his provider role seriously, he takes his time management seriously. Each decade of a man's life should be a level up from the last decade. When a man is in his teens and twenties, he should be working towards a planned-money-making-path by his thirtieth birthday. When he turns forty, he should be onto a new capstone of expansion. Think about life in an expanded view. A man's daily habits contribute to his future path. Each day should be like a step up on the ladder of accomplishment. If a man spends all his time watching mind numbing sports while getting drunk, then he will just turn into an old sport-watching-drunk. The only thing that will change in his life will be added wrinkles, an enlarged prostate and more useless stats in his head.

To plan for the future, a man must take his present seriously. A successful man is a man who has successful habits. The worse habits a man has, the worse circumstance he will have in the end. Early life is a preparation for end-of-life decay. Sound bleak? It isn't when a man is on his mission for glory. Because each man has an opportunity in touching the sun before his wave rolls to shore. Make the ride worth the trip. And it starts with daily and weekly discipline. By being disciplined, a man tells not only his woman that he has self-belief, but he reaffirms his own internal belief of self.

The guys who tend to be most in touch with their sexuality as teens and with the most access to it tend to suffer as a result. They get all the sex up front and so do not use their sex drive for self-betterment. These types of men age just as poorly as women. Their lack of drive will accumulate as they age and will deprive them of the dignity that is necessary for healthy masculine pride. When they hit forty and edge into fifty, they will start getting cucked by the same men they previously cucked in their youth. A woman as she ages wants to feel provided for and wants the dignity that money provides. That is why it is crucial for a young man to make his career path his top concern. Women will come and go but how a man provides for himself will stay with him to the end. Even in a relationship a man should always place his work above his woman because without his work she will place another man above him.

In our modern feminist age, we are seeing more men assume household duty while their dominant women provide for them. These men have sacrificed their dignity for the illusion of unframed "enlightenment" and have learned to fetishize their own weakness in order to preserve their egos. These relationships hold massive amounts of emasculation behind closed doors. The sex schedule is set by the woman because she has the reins of power and it dies under her control. While the man folds her underwear, she unfolds thoughts of another stronger man. The unframed man from his innate humiliation will be twisted with passive aggression. These men represent the failure of female leadership. When a woman becomes the dominant in a relationship, she becomes a tyrant who lacks compassion. Most times these relationships fall apart to infidelity.

The wall provides a woman her own virtue of spirit which allows her to exist outside of her feminine tyranny. The wall provides resource, and both receive dignity in return.

The

wall

holds

back

chaos

    When a woman is outside a man's masculine frame she will be plagued with anxiety and fear. The anxiety and fear will mix with her unstable emotional frame to form hysteria. Hysteria is when a woman gets caught in her own irrationality-loop because she lacks a man's calm rational certainty to break it. This psychologically damaged state creates further hysteria and panic. It is a snowball effect of mental illness from a lack of anchoring to reality. When the number of women who are unpaired from men's masculine frames rises in a society so does mental illness. When a woman is alone or with an unframed man, she will lose herself in her own emotional mind.

    A society that is feminized is a society that is on the brink of total chaos. The unframed state pushes men to over-reaction, option-paralysis and irrational decision making. The importance of picking up frame goes beyond the individual. A man who picks up masculine frame becomes like a human sandbag against the floods of feminine chaos. We each need to plug the hole of chaos together. Weak men for generations have abandoned masculine frame and have created our feminized modern world. When a tribe loses sense of masculinity it is in decay and fall. The sexual revolution was a massive shrug of masculinity and was a gunshot into the belly of civilization and it's been staggering in death throes ever since.

Men keep order and bring sanity to expansion. Despair overwhelms the common man's mind because he is weak and unframed. Did our ancestors despair when they failed to provide meat for their starving women and children back in the cave? Or did they become stronger because they were depended on. A man cannot afford to surrender to weak-willed defeatism. Leave pessimism to women and children who sacrifice little in making a sour note known. A man keeps the frame of glory shining not because he is a fool but because he knows his light must shine for those under his frame.

When my heart broke and the abandonment tallied into one of many abandonments in my life, did I let despair paralyze me in its tight grip?

I will not let chaos win, and neither should you. I don't care if your life has been only shit until now. We rise together because we believe in being men. And a man must overcome all obstacles in his path. Why? Because that is why we were spit out into existence. We are men and we bring order to chaos and light to darkness. We spark fire in the night to not only heat our food but to ease the minds of those afraid of the dark. We cure anxiety and fear with our willpower and optimism. Why be optimistic? Because to surrender is to castrate our balls in defeat. We carry with us our manhood and our belief in success. If I can muster belief in myself then why shouldn't you? Belief is the greatest power on this goddamn speck of dust we live on and it allows humanity to breathe deeply in our collective lung. Chaos only seems overwhelming to unframed spirits. Picture a glass half full and eventually your cup will run over. Close your eyes and believe in whatever being inhabits you beneath each eyelid. Life is too short and cruel to spend time lacking self-belief.

When a man becomes humiliated from a woman's disrespect is a disorder of nature. If a society collapses the first thing to go will be feminism and weak men. Civilization is an illusion of established order. Our forefathers built a civilization that gave false entitlement to women and their unframed men. Feminism only exists because men allowed it to exist. Feminism only exists because men have died for a woman's right to humiliate them. Feminism only exists because hard working men maintain the infrastructure that powers a feminist's computer which allows her to spread her masculine hatred online. And from this entitled position feminists have been working hard to spread decay in the very civilization that allowed it to blossom forth.

This behavior is the same as a woman who cheats on her weak provider. Women by nature bite the hand that feeds them because they are agents of chaos. Just as Eve followed her heart right out of paradise and her weak man followed behind her. When an environment is most accommodating to women is when they will be compelled to destroy it. Sound irrational? That is because it is. The feminization of society trains minds for irrationality. A woman would rather spark chaos than be bored by order. She both craves stability and resents it once it is achieved. That is the dual state of a woman's spirit. Just as she wants power over a man in a relationship but resents it as soon as it is in her hands.

This is the state of all things. Men build and women destroy. *Order and Chaos.* Growth and decay. In a way, it is as if a woman fights like hell to take the wheel from man only to crash the car. A grand gesture of showing that the responsibility was too much to bear and that the man was the fool to allow it. And he was.

To reestablish order, we must be willing to take the wheel of civilization from women before more damage is done. Many men have already learned the lesson of feminine resentment towards power and how cruelly women punish men who allow their own weakness in romance. A woman doesn't magically become a different person outside a romantic relationship. Power is power. One is small scale while the other large. The rationale remains the same.

When a man picks up masculine frame in a relationship, the power dynamic will flip to what is natural. He rises, she kneels. When each man takes back power in romance and makes his woman denounce feminism is when we will send feminism back into the abyss. It starts with each individual man and it spreads from there. The reason we exist in a feminist world is because men lack power in romance and have zero influence on a woman's belief system. When a woman is under a man's frame, she believes what he believes. The leader shows her the pleasure of feminine submission and the sex will prove it. Sex sells. That is the main reason that most men want to pick up masculine frame, to get laid.

When women experience the sex of a framed relationship they will happily forget about feminism and its sexual dysfunction. This book is the antidote to modern sexual dysfunction and helps men to align themselves with nature and to free them from the feminist lies they were sold from childhood. When each man makes his woman kneel in submissive pleasure is when we will see feminism fall.

183

The

wall

is

peace

Violence should never be the first option. When a man's power of negotiation fails, he will resort to force. In his mind he thinks, "If she will not respect my words then she will respect my fist." Does she respect such a man? No, this only stifles her own speech into internal sourness and resentment. A woman knows that a man must rely on violence not because he is strong but because all his other means have failed him. Masculine frame is not tyranny. If a man uses violence to control a woman, he abandons his masculinity to do so. Frame is self-control, not loss of temper. When I was younger, I was surrounded by men who ruled with fear not inspiration. "Cross me and pay." What effect did this have on me? I became ultra-agreeable in fear and abandoned my dignity to survive. I learned not to cross these men while despising their tyranny in my heart. If a man inspires resentment, he inspires his future downfall. When a man is practicing masculine frame correctly, he inspires others to follow his lead not because they fear him but because they genuinely respect his example.

A woman is submissive to the wall not because the wall pushes her down on her knees but because the wall inspires her knees to touch ground. There is the expression to be a "Man of one's word", which is used to associate honesty with masculinity, but the expression goes further to signify the power of a man's word in authority. He commands and a woman obeys. She obeys not from fear of violence but from fear of letting her leader down. When a woman is under a masculine frame, she falls into submission to better compliment the man in the relationship.

When a man uses his fist, he lets the woman know his words are impotent. She doesn't listen to him because she doesn't respect him and beating her won't change that. Forcing respect with violence is like cleaning house by sweeping dirt under rugs. Everything becomes hidden and outside a man's view of perception. If a man hits a woman, he knocks her clear out of his knowing. She will be more secretive because she must protect herself. To hit a woman is to surrender to weak compulsion. The man of violence is a tyrant, and we all cheer for his eventual fall.

A man ruled by violence is like a bull raging to a matador's cape. He becomes reactive like a predictable animal and can be gamed by others. Being able to turn away from impulsive thoughts is proof of human intelligence.

"But Jerr," a voice calls out from off the page, "When someone humiliates me in public, I have to stick up for my pride and don't want to be a coward."

Do we say, "what a brave bull" when it plows mindlessly forward or do, we say "what a powerfully simple-minded beast?"

To hold back anger is a sign of intelligence because it signals a man understands consequences which means he can look past "matadors' capes" that flash in his view. Ignoring taunts is not cowardly but rather proof a man is wise to tactic. The main issue with violent men is that they are over-reactive to other's frame of reality. *To ignore a person is to view yourself above them.* To engage is to agree that they are equals if not masters. Non-reaction is the glue that holds frame together. A man is not dependent on others validation of his bravery or cowardice. If he must act, he will act but he will not react. When a man over-reacts to another person is because he overly believes in their reality. To ignore another is to lack belief in another as authority.

When a man is worrying about whether he needs to react to disrespect, first he must judge the value of the issuer of disrespect. For example, if I were walking home from work and a random stranger insulted me, I would keep walking. Why? Because who is this stranger to me that I should care enough to engage? See the rationale? Care-enough-to-engage. Before a man defends his honor, first he must admit that the one telling him to prove it is valid in the request.

Raging bull type men need to see violence for what it is, childish force. When a man throws a punch at a woman, he throws out his dignity as well. These types of men need to work on impulse control and charisma. Charisma is how a man can walk away from conflict with his dignity intact. Charisma preserves dignity. When a man uses his speech to settle matters, he proves that his words hit harder than his fists. Let speech and removal of presence be the control mechanisms within the relationship. If words fail then remove presence. And if a woman will not submit then a man should stay gone. That is how masculine men have controlled their environments for millennia: By threat of their absence of resource and potential resource. A woman only learns to respect based on fear-of-loss. If a man creates an environment where a woman would not fear his loss, then that is his fault.

A raging bull type man creates an environment of fear and anxiety which will eventually catch up to him. Tyrants always fall. When a man uses violence instead of his masculine frame, what he is telling himself and his woman is that he does not believe in his frame enough to stand by it. The frame is enough, and a woman knows it. By punching holes in walls and throwing lamps, a man is showing his fear of loss of control. *A man needs to overcome his fear and not surrender to it.* If a man genuinely believed in his leadership, then he would not result to weak fear tactics. The wall is peace because a man is at peace with himself.

187

The

wall

knows

By now my reader will see how much rationalization goes on behind a man's wall of masculinity. A man acts in a framed way not from dull-headed posturing but for his own dignity in the swamp of human nature. We live in a world of chaos and confusion. We make the best of what we have, and just because we have a shit hand doesn't mean we need to fold. To expect perfection is to expect disappointment. When an unframed man becomes emotionally dependent on his woman, he will idolize her with an image of angelic morality. That is why unframed men hurt so badly when their idealistic fantasy comes crashing down from their heavenly expectation into the hell of how-things-really-are.

A framed man knows women better than they know themselves, just as a fisherman knows fish. Even with the level of knowledge of their imperfection he does not call it quits with these devious creatures. No, he tightens his frame and keeps his wall up. Two things must be understood. One, that women innately veer towards chaos and secondly, that the wall helps to prevent chaos. That doesn't mean that the wall will prevent chaos in a man's life completely, only that the wall encourages a woman to be in order. And the wall protects the man from emotional hurt from a woman's chaotic nature. To appreciate a lion a man must appreciate the sharpness of its tooth and claw otherwise what he is appreciating is nothing but fantasy.

To appreciate women, a man must appreciate them for what they truly are otherwise what he is appreciating is a falsehood. That false image is what allows unframed men to be exploited while setting them up for heartbreak. Picking up frame is to admit the necessity of it for a relationship like the chair in a lion tamer's hand. When a framed man sees a man being unframed, he sees the "nice guy" putting himself in dangerous and foolish scenarios with women. A woman should always be kept at an emotional distance otherwise she will punish the man for letting down his wall.

"But Jerr," a voice calls out from off the page, "But for love to exist doesn't the man need to be vulnerable?"

A man loves a woman when he lets down his wall and starts becoming emotional like a woman. Love is for women. A man can love a woman to a degree, but all the emotional energy should be on the woman's side. The wall itself compels a woman to feel in love because women need a wall to reach that level. A woman does not fall in love with a man's personality, she falls in love with the wall that hides his personality. To expect anything different is like expecting a lion to act like a lamb. Love women for what they are, women. There is nothing womanlier than a woman falling head-over-heels for a wall. If a man genuinely loved women, then he would keep the wall up for them. It is when a man falls in love with himself that he abandons frame. A man getting emotional over a woman is him falling in love with the *idea of love*. That is what romantic types do, they fall in love not with a woman but with themselves falling in love with a woman.

To allow a woman to be the one who is in love within a relationship comes from a true place of love hidden behind a man's wall. That is the reason why women fall in love with walls and not the men hiding behind walls. The wall is representative of what a man sacrifices for his woman. To be framed is caring while being unframed is selfish. Another reason why women feel little guilt in punishing a man outside his wall.

A framed man knows the wall is necessary for a woman's wellbeing because outside a man's wall a woman is a more devious creature. The wall protects a woman from herself. Outside masculine frame, women become crueler than even they could have imagined. Masculine frame is the dam against the floods of their chaos. Unframed men expect perfection from women and cry when women fail to match their absurd expectations. To know a woman is to be aware of a woman's innate disloyalty. She is a walking erogenous zone with irrational emotions bouncing around in her heart. She is equal parts existential terror and equal parts opportunist to a passing king. When a high value man enters a room with a woman her body becomes a lightning rod to his magnetism. She melts like butter on his toast. A common excuse when a woman is disloyal is that she "lost herself." This usually is seen as a woman shrugging accountability but also it speaks truth to feminine existence. Women do lose themselves to unfaithfulness. But they didn't "lose themselves" in the sense they believe, they "revealed themselves" and it frightened them. The effect of a prized man taking interest in a woman puts her into sexual heat. A woman fears most not cashing on her beauty while she still has it. She knows that her age and beauty will eventually fade and so when a "good catch" enters her life, a woman's brain will shut off and she will jump at the opportunity to change her world. Even if this means being disloyal to her current man.

Older generations used to think of infidelity as being what men did, but our modern times have shown us that women perpetrate infidelity more than men while unframed men cry about relationship stability. Not all women are physically disloyal, but all women are emotionally disloyal to a degree. A woman will flirt with disaster because she is a chaos agent by nature. Nothing is more common than women seeking other men's attention while they are in a relationship. A woman will flirt and play around with her feelings over a work crush. This is pornography to women. Unlike pornography, this is flirtation with reality, not stagnant like fantasy. Also, a woman has more access to sex because she needs only to surrender whereas a man must work to make a woman desire to surrender. Sexual selection is a woman's game because to a woman, to surrender is to win.

With the vast rise of unframed men in modern society it is no wonder women have given themselves over to more romantic chaos. They do not worry about "losing themselves" because without a frame they already feel lost. They trespass on to unholy land because they already feel dead. Outside of a man's masculine frame a woman becomes desperate and cruel. The sooner a man realizes that his woman will cheat on him, the sooner he will be able to let go of this unframed idea of feminine loyalty. When an unframed man puts a woman on a moral pedestal, he creates feelings of self-loathing in her. She cannot rise above her own negative behavior and his hopes only further remind her of how she falls short. The only thing a man asks of his woman is to be sexually faithful because he knows it will be near impossible for her to be emotionally faithful. If a woman cheats on a man and becomes physical with another she signals to her man and the entire tribe that his genetic material is inferior. A man cheating is like a slap while a woman cheating is like murder. Both are wrong but vastly different. This level of humiliation is too much for a man's masculine pride to bear and to protect his dignity he must abandon the woman even if she crawls back to his cave.

"But Jerr," a voice calls out from off the page, "If women are cheaters by nature and will cheat no matter what we do, isn't that depressing?"

The more a man is unframed the more depressing it will feel. Remember that expecting a woman to be a woman and enjoying her for what she truly is calms a man. He doesn't expect an angel and therefore is less disturbed by falls from glory. When a man understands a woman's innate disloyal nature he understands that dealing with women is a shared experience among all men. Men who want to be in relationships with women have to deal with their unfaithfulness, men high up the class ladder and men low in class. All men experience the humiliations of betrayal but with this understanding comes a solidarity. Think about it like this, we men are lion tamers who love lions, and our scars don't build hate for the beasts we want to interact with. We know there is danger in the game.

The reason I am writing this book is, the level of masculine humiliation is rising to fever pitch and our state of indignity must be rectified. The rise of fatherlessness has created generations of orphaned boys that grew up into feminine dominated men. These men loathe themselves and respect the feminine as pure and holy. They need to flip the script in their mind that they were indoctrinated with. *We are going to empower men because we believe in men.* I believe in myself and I expect you to do the same. Don't give up hope on yourself and don't give up hope on women. Alter expectations and do not see a woman's emotional disloyalty as heartbreaking.

"But Jerr," a shaking voice cries out, "HOW???"

Become framed. It is a man's unframed state that opens him up to the trauma and pain of a broken heart. When a man exists above emotion, he looks upon the world with rational eyes. The state of being framed is to be above emotions that drag us down. A woman cannot help but be controlled by her emotions, but a man can work on controlling his own. We are built for it. The problem with an unframed man is his need for emotional validation. His emotions twist inside him and he relies on his woman to untwist his internal chaos. When an unframed man is looking for a best friend in romance, what he is wanting is a mother figure. He wants the woman to exist above his emotions and help him navigate his doubts and fears. This is selfish because it is the woman who needs the most help with emotional guidance.

By not depending on a woman emotionally, a man is able to keep enough distance needed for his leadership which also protects him from the emotional trauma of her chaos. If a man is framed, then a woman cannot get close enough to stab his heart with an emotional dagger.

"But Jerr," a voice calls out from off the page, "Don't you believe in love?"

I believe in love and my belief helps me to create the needed environment for a woman to achieve that emotion. Also, to believe in something, first it must be defined. "Love" is an undefinable word and means as much as someone wants it to. Do I have feelings of love within me? The wall is proof of that. Because by keeping frame I am showing with my actions my love for a woman. When an unframed man cries and moans about his love for his woman but then cruelly shrugs frame and depends on her emotionally, to me that is not loving. *To love a woman is to provide her with masculine frame.* To love yourself is to abandon frame in order to preserve personality. An unframed man thinks he loves a woman because he is lost in his emotions which he refuses to control.

A man carrying frame is like a surfer on the waves of chaos. He stays above it but if he looked down, he might be overwhelmed by what is under him. Stay above and do not sink. That is what it means to be a man, to stay above what drags down women. They are emotional wrecks who crave an emotionally stable being to help them calm themselves. If a man becomes overwhelmed by his emotions, his woman will see this as a masculinity breakdown.

A woman punishes all masculinity breakdowns. Frame breaks reveal not controlled vulnerability but loss of control of what makes us vulnerable. When a man cries, even if they are tears of love for his woman, she will see it for what it truly is, emotional dependence. And a woman will punish a man for any dependent behavior even if it is professed to be love. To be a man is rejecting the need for dependence on a woman. A woman rewards what does not need her. That is the key to understanding women. They love cats because they love being around a creature that is not dependent on them. A woman will try her hardest to make it seem like a cat is dependent with all kinds of comfort purchases, but the beast could make it just as easy on the street. An animal like a dog is a true dependent and women will easily fall into resentment over caring for them. A man should be more like a cat and less like a dog. It is the needing of validation that women despise. When a man doesn't need validation for his self, this projects independence which is required in a leader.

To be "in love" with a woman is to be in fear of losing her and a man must never fear the loss of his woman. As soon as the fear is projected to her then she will fall "in love" with another man. That is the cruel twist of reality that we must all understand. A man should control his emotions and project strength always to his woman, that is if he truly "loves" her.

Outside

the

wall:

Three

unframed

archetypes

My two brothers and I were raised by a dominant mother. Our personalities split into three unframed archetypes that are widely seen from fatherless men or men with weak fathers. This understanding comes partially from my own observation mixed with readings of Freud and Jung. The three archetypes are like three animals each under a different stress of survival. These "animal" types have defective psychology due to their stress instinct being irrationally stuck on. The first animal is the raging bull type. He is the bad boy, ladies' man and fighter. This man is stuck in fight mode and deals with life from impulse rather than rationality. The next is the flighty bird type. This man is the sensitive type usually seen as a "dandy" sometimes homosexual (my brother is not) and most in his feminine frame, he redirects (takes to flight) his sexual selection away from women and seeks out sex most like his own image which comes from his over identification with the mother. He is stuck in flight mode and fetishizes his redirection of spirit.

The last is my type, the paralyzed deer. This type is like a deer caught and frozen in the headlights of life. I'm the neurotic type that has lived a good portion of my life seized by fear. My type has more issues with mustering bravery for action and falls on the opposite spectrum of the raging bull. (Raging bulls don't tend to be writers because when my type was reading books they were out fighting and fucking.) My type's frozen state has primed me for being more observant of others. While they act, I watch. That is one reason that paralyzed deer type men have higher intelligence while falling victim to voyeurism. It comes from being stuck within their bodies and minds.

If a man is paying enough attention, he will recognize these types all around. Three unframed men with three different unframed problems. With the rise of single mothers ruling over the psychology of growing young men we will see a rise in defective men's psychology from the stress-of-survival instinct being triggered and stuck on.

A father's frame cures each one of their unframed states. To be stuck in fight, flight and freeze is to remain an animal. This animal complex keeps men from achieving the success in sexual selection that rising above their individual survival stress would provide. They each need to transcend the animal complex and break free from their broken state of fear. The raging bull and flighty bird both have a fear of inaction but separated in difference, one runs towards, the other away while the paralyzed deer fears action itself. All three are reactionary but in each a unique way.

"But Jerr," a voice calls out from outside the page, "Isn't a man's homosexuality genetic and not psychological?"

The "born this way" rhetoric is over simplified and dismisses any suggestion at a psychological reason for homosexuality. While a small part could come from a man's genetic makeup, most likely a man's upbringing and early experiences have shaped his sexual selection decisioning. Because why the hell not? "Born this way" is an easy way to shrug any accountability for lifestyle. It is a permissive way to view reality. This accountability shrug is celebrated by women because they cannot help but agree with any philosophy that shrugs personal responsibility.

On a personal level, I do not care what a man does with his own body. But to say that homosexuality is purely genetic and not psychological is simple-minded. The reason why the "born this way" narrative is being sold is to silence opposition to the possible dangers of mass psychological influence. The narrative of genetic over psychological is to calm parents into submission from worrying about their children being influenced by association and propaganda. This narrative quells the societal worry. But if homosexuality is based on psychological factors, then propagation of gender fluidity acceptance would have a psychological impact on growing minds open to suggestion. This discussion on whether homosexuality is nature or nurture should not be silenced for politically correct reasons. The proponents of "born this way" are acting in good faith to protect homosexuals from persecution and violence. They push an over simplified narrative in condescension to control the masses which they view as simple minded brutes. *Violence and hate should never be celebrated.* But to sell falsehood while denying societal impact is foolish. Fatherless boys who are surrounded by gender fluid celebration only further confuses these young men into abandoning masculinity which increases the power transfer from men to women in society.

For each animal type the father's frame is the cure. He cures the boys of their animal complex by pulling them out of their stress response with his frame. Rationality to the raging bull, masculine responsibility to the flighty bird and assertive confidence to the paralyzed deer. Masculine frame helps each transcend the stress-of-survival state. Once a man is out of his survival mode, he can conquer reality and not be gamed by reality like an animal.

PROJECT

WEAKNESS AND

INSPIRE INFIDELITY

IN YOUR WOMAN

Testing

walls

When a man is around other masculine men, he will notice that they will "bust each other's balls" by calling attention to each other's emotional weak spots. If a guy is fat, his friends will call him "lard ass," if a guy is bald, they will call him "cue ball" and so forth. While females are sensitive to language, men will playfully test each other with bold and offensive speech. Why? What does it mean to get emotional over someone calling us a name? It means we believe in their authority over us. It means we surrender our self-belief to their perception and abandon our frame. This is the core rationale for shit testing. Men test each other because they are testing each other's *sense of self.* If a man can easily be made angry by others perception, he does not truly believe in his own authority. To believe other people's opinion of ourselves is to doubt our own opinion of ourselves. Why would men "bust balls"? It is leadership training. Men innately groom each other for the high emotional stress of leadership positions. We only want to follow someone who has a strong sense of self and who cannot easily be made to doubt themselves. This is why masculine men use offensive speech to attempt to trigger each other into emotionalism. When a man understands it as a game, he can detach himself from the vulgar testing and see it for what it is. But the key thing about busting balls is that it requires us to be calm in reception while being calm in giving it back. If a man just takes abuse from other men, he will be seen as passive and they will become emboldened over him which will cause them to bully the weakness even further. If a man laughs off a verbal attack and then gives it back, he is seen as strong. If the other guy gives but cannot take it is a failure of his own masculine frame. When I was unframed growing up and no one explained this to me; I would become passive when being verbally bullied and would not give it back. This only antagonized the men who were trying to find a weak point in my psychological armor. When a man becomes passive, he is failing the game which puts a negative spotlight back on the men trying to be playful. He himself has made the playful sparring serious which irritates the men into further bullying him. Offensive language is a core of masculine frame because we use language to test each other's passivity and emotionalism. Call a woman fat and she will doubt herself in emotional breakdown. Call a man fat and he will laugh before pointing out your own weak spot. This is all part of the game of ball busting. Why would we want to associate with men who lack a strong sense of self? Men who can easily be made to doubt themselves fail as leaders and they fail as someone we could depend on in a high stress event. They crumble over speech which begs the question on what else they would crumble over. All shit testing is testing the integrity of our sense of self and how we are affected by others attempts to gain authority over us. A person will look for a weak spot to see how a man handles the pressure of doubt placed on him.

A woman is designed to test a man's confidence in his frame. She will test him until he is dead. Men who become emotional and angry over testing will only showcase a weakness that compels their women to test them further in the future. The weakness will increase her anxiety and will make her doubt her man's sense of self. This is why the more a man fails shit tests with a woman in a relationship, the more she will be compelled to test him. He shows her the chink in his armor and she must further dig into the weak spot. Why? Because she must reassure herself of his sense of self if she is going to allow him to impregnate her with that sense. She wants to carry a proud and strong child in her womb which requires her to make sure the father is strong and proud. But not all women are equal in the degree that they test men. For example, if a woman is fatherless or had a father who was passive growing up, she will be more apt to shit test men because men have made her paranoid about trusting their authority. The more women were failed by masculine authority, the more doubt they will carry over a man's masculine frame. This means that a fatherless woman will feel the need to test her man until she become reassured. This means that she will make more vulgar attempts at humiliating him and will test more often. But just because she requires more energy in framing does not mean that she is hopeless. All women can be framed by a man but a man may not want to frame a particular woman. It is dependent on what he gains from placing so much energy on a female who requires more work. This is up the individual man to decide for himself. A man should realize that a woman who is "testy" is a woman looking for reassurance. She holds high anxiety over her trust in male authority which means she must reassure herself with high amount of testing to ease that doubt. If a man sees it this way can help him in calmly passing tests by immediately standing up for his dignity and by correcting the female. This will help him to stay rational. Why? He will understand that he would only become emotional because her testing is revealing a weakness that he is afraid to admit to himself. If someone's speech makes us emotional, they have gained authority over us. It is a revelation of doubt over our own self-belief. Knowing this helps us to play the game without letting the game play us. Remember that testing is natural to our human species. Do not take it too seriously and do not passively allow others to humiliate you.

Unwalled

faces

A man who is in masculine circles in our times will encounter memes about "soy face." This is when nerdy guys make exaggerated facial expressions into a camera lens for pictures. Their eyes will be wide open and their mouths will be wide open. They are attempting to display an uncontained emotional exuberance. In this chapter, I will discuss the psychological reasons why a generation of "soy boys" make these goofy faces and the reasons for their behavior.

When an infant is first learning to read faces, his mother will make wide facial expressions in exaggeration to reassure the infant's emotions. As we age, we gain a nuanced capacity for reading faces and behaviors. But at the early start of our lives, we will be easily confused by the hidden intent in others. This is why a baby can be made to cry by a person making a frown or angry face at it just as a baby can be made to smile. Infants are ultra-sensitive to the faces we make at them. When a mother is making wide-eyed and wide-mouthed faces to her infant, she is opening up her face to reveal that she is not hiding intent from the baby. It is like she is revealing all the cards in her hand in the game of poker. It is a reassurance that there is no bluff to her intent. When we get older, we are able to have a strong enough sense of self that allows us to not be controlled by the negative emotions of others. A moody person will not infect us with their moodiness. But a baby does not have this independent sense of self yet and becomes dependent on a reassurance of emotion.

When men are in their feminine frame, they will become like infants in easy disturbance to other's emotional states. Remember, a nice guy is nice because he infantilizes others and himself. He knows that he is emotionally sensitive which makes him view others as emotionally sensitive from empathy. He acts "nice" in condescension to others because he wants to be treated that way. When a group of "nice guys" or "soy boys" get around each other, they will be high on emotional reassurance. They will make an effort to reassure each other that they are not hiding ill intent. This is why they make exaggerated gestures of emotionally reassuring behaviorism. It comes from an internal weakness and a projection of that weakness onto others. They make faces wide in harmless expressions to reassure each other that they are not hiding negative emotions. What they do not realize is that they are infantilizing each other and are being condescending to each other's lack of capacity for nuance. Their over nurturing behaviorism is to protect the weakness they perceive in others which only further weakens what they aim to protect. Their faces become wide open in harmless display because they themselves are easily triggered into negative emotion. They end up behaving in bizarre infantilized gestures as a way to "walk on eggshells" around those given to emotional disturbance. When a man is practicing masculine frame, he is hiding his intent from others which triggers their imaginations. What could a blank face be thinking? This is why female love to fantasize about framed men. It allows them to use their imaginations. But infantilized men will not use their internal doubt for sexual arousal but rather grow in fear to the threat of the other male. And when a man is practicing frame, he will allow himself to show "micro expressions" which allows nuance and belief in the maturity of those reading his face. A framed man has a strong sense of self that is not easily disturbed by the facial expressions of others and he does not coddle others by acting like a mother to a baby with his own facial expressions. He allows himself to hide his own intent and he does not depend on others being completely open with their own intent. How do you feel when someone frowns at you? Does it make you doubt yourself? Does it make you become emotionally disturbed? A baby is hyper sensitive to the faces of others because he lacks a strong sense of self. "Soy boys" make exaggerated faces to each other because they have a weak sense of self which they are trying to protect from other's doubt. This is why a man must realize that infantilizing other men with wide open expressions is a condescension to their inner power. We coddle others when we doubt their ability to survive in an environment. Emotional coddling is arrogant to the capacity of strength we all hold. "Soy boys" act as mother hens to the emotional needs of each other because they refuse to grow up. They cling to action figures and cartoons with wide expression because they feel safe in an adolescence they refuse to surrender. Stop making baby faces to your friends and stop expecting the world to treat you like a baby. This is frame.

Worshipping

other

walls

When a generation of men are in their feminine frame of authority, fatherless and have been raised to doubt themselves; they will be more conditioned to hero worship.

When I was unframed, I remember using "authority placeholders" to bolster my opinion on reality. This comes from chronic self-doubt. A man will tell his woman something and when she doubts him, he will say "This other guy said so" as if that proves his own view of reality. Listen closely, when a man's frame is strong enough, he can make the rules and others join his game. He does not need to place others as trustworthy authority figures to give confidence to his own speech. *What my reader must understand is that I have zero to gain from discouraging hero worship.* This is why most "heroes" of our time never tell their audience to stop worshiping them. They benefit from men giving away their own power. These men stand atop the pyramid of power and relish the fact that they are surrounded by men bowing down before them. They could tell them to stand up, but they rarely do.

When I was unframed, I remember having a fascination with so called female male empowerment writers. Women who debated other feminists and who encouraged men to have pride. Looking back, I realize that I was giving them my power and allowing them to speak for me was further strengthening the feminine frame of authority in my own mind. This generation of men who hold tremendous doubt in their own authority will be more prone to lift up others as mouthpieces for them.

A man who lacks a strong father figure will be more suggestible in seeking out father figures to replace the one he never had. A loving father is one who transfers power to his son. He wants a son who is equally proud as him and he encourages the rebellion that eventually allows independence. Why? Because a father who truly loves his son wants him to have a better life than he had. He wants him to be stronger and prouder than he was. Weak fathers keep their sons in their authority because they fear giving away power. They fear losing control and so they hold tightly to the secrets of their authority.

Men who are in their feminine frame of authority will hold doubt over their own power and will be conditioned for submission. This means that in our last days of hyper feminization, we will see a rise of "masculine heroes" who are everything that this weak generation of men want to be. These masculine heroes will exude machismo with asshole charisma. They will showcase their muscles and wealth for other men to celebrate. Live action voyeurism and a virtual reality of life. Men will vicariously live their fantasies through these heroes. The heroes flaunt their physique and sexual adventures to their followers who passively enjoy the fruits of these modern-day kings. Weak men believe that by worshiping strength, they will somehow absorb what makes these men great. But what they do not realize is that the belief in one's own power is what makes these men great. These men do not worship other men, they worship themselves. Do their followers know this? No. They are too deeply under the spell of father figures they never had. They are too entranced by the spell of unbounded male empowerment that they do not realize they are in an audience to another man's show. This forgotten generation have been conditioned into cuckold behaviorism. They passively watch as men live life for them. Voyeurs to other men playing sports. Voyeurs to other men fucking women. All they know is submission and passivity. All they know is to surrender their authority to others.

Another issue with the rise of hero worship is that there are homo erotic implications. A lot of "masculine heroes" will showcase attractive elements of their lives whether muscles, money or cars which are the core elements that make females attracted to them. But this weak generation join in celebrating the fruits of these men's success as if that is normal. It is as if these weak men are like salesmen to the sexual pleasure of another. They stand clapping at the showy display of achievement of their heroes which is like them handing away pussy to these heroes. Why would a man celebrate another man's muscles and wealth? Why would a man celebrate another man's sexual escapades? It is a form of cuckoldry. But this generation are so full of self-loathing and conditioned into feminine submission that they applaud in others what they should be applauding in themselves. They give away power because they fear it in their own hands. Listen closely, it does not matter if another guy has bigger muscles and less fat; *your smaller muscles are better.* Men that obsess over their own showy display are puffing up their self-belief for validation. But it is all in the mind. It is all attitude. A man can be fat or scrawny with more confidence than a man with muscles. My pile of dirt is better than another man's pile of gold. I want you to be proud as hell. I do not want to see this orphaned generation being led into worship to a few heroes only because they lack what it means to believe in themselves.

What a man must realize is that a woman can be with a loser but will be loyal to his frame. The world is full of losers who think they are hot stuff. And their self-belief tricks their women into that same frame of thought. A female feels safe in a man's ego. The frame of his own self-belief is what makes her aroused. Remember, a young child will think that their father is a superhero even if he is a janitor. It is the frame that matters. If man is constantly pointing to other men in admiration while never inspiring admiration himself, he robs himself of inspiring others to have confidence in his authority. Men who point to heroes as placeholders for their own self-respect are disrespecting themselves. Admire their work but do not idolize them. We appreciate hard work and talent but we do not view fellow men as perfect. This is the core difference between admiration and hero worship. It is whether we appreciate a man's creation or whether we focus our admiration on the man himself.

But there is something more insidious to the hero worship of our times. When men are feminized and are accustomed to submission, they will identify with female's arousal in sexual selection. They become aroused by masculine heroes because the machismo is stimulating to the weakness that exists within them. There is a deep homo erotic element to men celebrating the bodies of other men. They will gaslight themselves into thinking it is merely admiration of discipline but we know there is something deeper to it.

A man acts like a princess in need of saving when he indulges in hero worship. Females are innately passive in sexual selection because they present themselves to high value men they want to attract. They merely need to be, whereas a man must become. The act of becoming is a hero's journey that requires us to each become a hero. It means we should not lift up other men as heroes but rather see ourselves as the hero in the story of our lives. I do not want to be your hero, I merely want to be your guide. YOU ARE THE HERO IN YOUR OWN LIFE. This generation of men have become passive and easily controlled by the will of others. We need less princesses in our world. We need more kings. If this generation of men had loving fathers, they would have been trained to see it as weak to lift up others as heroes. Remember, if a man believes himself to be the hottest thing on earth, women will feel the heat. It is all mojo. When we have "masculine heroes," we give away our mojo like cucks. View yourself as the equal of all men. View me as a guide to your own heroism. Never point pussy to another cock. Do not give your energy away to a man who could care less if you exist.

The

wall

is

serious

To be treated like a king a man must act like a king. When a man plays the part of fool, he shouldn't be surprised when he is treated as such. An unframed man is emotionally attached to his personality because he uses it to receive affection. If someone does not approve of his personality, he becomes depressed and anxious. This puts a man in a validate-to-others mindset and not expect-others-to-validate to him mindset. A king lets those around his throne dance for attention, not the reverse.

For a man to take his masculinity seriously, he must take himself seriously. This is the starting point. And it sets the tone for how he wants to be treated. A fool only shows more foolishness when he stops his silliness to demand respect. Nobody respects clowns and a man only further encourages his own humiliation by acting like one.

The reason an unframed man lacks dignity is he is dependent on others for his self-belief. A stand-up comic is only as funny as the laughs he gets from his audience. When the crowd becomes silent his spirit disappears within him. Why? Because he is in validation mode and requires an audience to validate his jokes and delivery. The sillier a man makes himself the more he is wanting to be loved, not respected. His attempts at buffoonery are to build affection not dignity. That is why a man should overcome his "silly persona" that he created in his youthful search for attention and love. A framed man wants respect, not love. Leave love and affection to weak men, women and children. To be framed is to be dependent on self alone for validation while in expectation of receiving respect.

When a man is raised by a woman alone, he will see her chasing affection. This "chasing affection" mode is womanly and should not be a mindset within a man. The wall needs to be serious because respect is a serious thing. When men start picking up frame, they might go from being called "Joey" to wanting to be called "Joseph." That is the start of a man seeking his own masculinity by distancing the new persona from the previous child persona that sought love over respect. When a man was a child, he would have been laughed at in fun because children are more in need of affection and validation. The day a man separates his boyhood from his manhood is when he himself chooses respect over love. But first a man must love himself enough to want to be respected. It is through self-love that a man wants to protect his dignity by seeking respect.

But here is where an unframed man gets confused. While being a goofball might create affection for himself, it only decreases the love a woman has for her man. Why? Because a woman falls "in love" with a man's own protection of his dignity. If a man robs himself of dignity, then what is there for her to fall in love

215

with? She might have affection, but it will be more familiar and less romantic. Everyday women cheat and divorce men they "love" but don't respect. In their hearts they see these men as "friends" or "like brothers" and not romance material. A woman falls in love with a man's wall, not his tap dance for affection.

These unframed men who act like fools in order to be loved need to first love themselves. They are uneasy in spirit because they were never given the tools for their own existence. People around them have exploited their lack of belief for their own gain in power. This is incredibly common to mankind. An exploiter will think "Look at this moron. I'll keep him around to inflate my own ego while mocking his lack of dignity. Other people will see me as more important and women will give me more notice because of this."

This exploiter is a leach on human dignity and hates his own masculinity by robbing his brother of it. Every single man on the planet deserves his own masculine pride. Too many men are getting left behind in this world because of the absence of father figures. We as orphans of mankind in our forgotten generation need to help each other up and not become leaches to others self-loathing.

An unframed man with a jester complex has social anxiety and tries to cure his own anxiety with validation approval acts. For example, if a man with a jester complex sat with a framed man it would be the jester who first breaks silence. He is under compulsion to ease the psychological suffering that comes from silence that robs him of approval. Men with a jester complex suffer most in silence because it robs them on the constant validation that they rely upon. This type of man feels compelled to be the savior to the uncomfortable by displaying his own uncomfortable state. This jester-type man makes jokes to relieve social tension. He acts in a way to ease the suffering of not only himself but others. The problem with this savior approach is calmness would be the better example for others and not expressed anxiety. A man's calm masculine frame sets an example of framed calmness for those with social anxiety. That is why a psychologist will have a certain calm demeanor to ease those with psychological difficulty into a frame of confidence. That frame-of-confidence does not speak because silence eases tension when it is accepted as normal. Jesters fear silence because it robs them of certainty-of-self. How can a jester be certain unless he drains others of their approval? That is why people will be emotionally exhausted around this type of man. He requires too much of their belief for his own self-belief.

"But Jerr," a voice calls out from off the page, "How does a man fix this part of his personality?"

He needs to destroy his personality and become a new man. He needs to go from a "Joey" to "Joseph" in his spirit. One way to help is to start standing up for dignity and let those that profess to love you get on board or not. It takes a man's backbone to protect his own dignity. Speak up when others try to make a fool of you and risk losing them. If someone doesn't want to respect you, then they are worth losing.

Another way a man can break his jester complex is to go into forced solitude for a time. This isolation will help him to learn to depend on his own validation and not others. Solitude is most helpful for his type of man. He needs to prove to himself that an audience isn't necessary for his own existence. He needs to work on expecting others to break silence to untrain his self-consciousness and social nervousness. Let the other person get nervous and break the silence. (This is not a permanent mindset only for temporary training.)

A jester-type man needs to untrain himself in his expectation of "needing a fool" in a room. Nobody needs a fool in a room. If anything, we need more proud frames in every room. When someone needs a fool in a room is because they want to exploit a fool in a room. It comes from a weakness within them to expect buffoonery in another. If someone is genuinely strong, then they would not require a pawn for laughing at.

Does that mean that a man never jokes? No, but he makes sure that he is not constantly the butt of jokes of others or makes others the butt of his jokes. It is not a man's job to make others laugh but sometimes he does because he wants to tell a funny joke. That should be a rarity and not part of his common personality. A man who is always telling jokes is a man who is always seeking validation which displays his level of emotional dependency.

Jester-type men repel women because women want king-like confidence from their men. But if a man of this type happens to be in a relationship with a woman, she will take on the role of serious leader for him and have deep resentment of his man-child state. The more a woman acts like the "adult in the room," the more she takes on a motherly role which robs her of her own feminine pleasure. Two people in a relationship cannot both be the "carefree one." Better for a woman to be in her carefree feminine than the man. The more serious a man becomes in his relationship the freer to be silly his woman will be. And she will reward him with respect and sex for this burden he carries for her.

These jester-type men as they age, and if they do not change, become either vengeful jokers or sad clowns. If they become **vengeful jokers**, it is because instead of changing they would rather pay back society though violence because of all the stacked humiliations that was previously given them. They preserved all the humiliations in passive aggression and their capacity for indignities overflows into uncontrolled wrath. These men have violent fantasies and dream of one final blood-soaked joke to tell the world.

The **sad clown** is a man with the jester complex who with age builds up his pathetic victimhood mindset and further seeks pity instead of changing himself. He exists like a living martyr to his pathetic condition and proves to the world their own rottenness by showcasing his humiliated state. He incites others to mock him only to further prove to himself that humanity is wicked. He would rather carry his victimology to the grave than to stand his ground for respect. He has fetishized his self-pity into a living act.

This shrugging of the seriousness of masculinity is a symptom of our times. At no other time have young fatherless boys been left to virtual fantasy while young women are prepped for real world leadership. These boys are forgotten to fantasies. They grow into men with infantilized taste in entertainment. And their need for constant entertainment is just as much as a child. They consume infantilizing entertainment in order to escape the difficulty of their own realities. They rely psychologically on entertainment as a security blanket over their fears. And no one benefits more from the infantilization of men than the feminist. While men lose themselves in fruitless pursuits that create this man-child state, women dominate the power structure of society. Why? Because a forgotten generation of men have been left to rot in this undignified state in order to be robbed of their authority. That is why feminists love comic books and encourage men to be in an eternal Peter Pan syndrome. They want these men to keep their security blankets in order to keep them weak. A woman easily procures power if the man willingly abandons it for fantasy. It is a massive shit test on a global scale. When men start taking their dignity seriously, they will push away the trivial pursuits that keep them in a slave state and start seeking power.

In the past, young boys were prepared as "future leaders." Those societies would see it as a real need to help men on their journey of masculinity. One such case is Theodore "Teddy" Roosevelt's 'Strength and decency' speech. It is a moving speech that was given in order to prepare young minds for masculine dignity and leadership. Teddy Roosevelt was a beautiful example of masculine pride and I recommend all men to read more about his fascinating and rugged life.

Instead of moving speeches about young men's future leadership we are currently in a modern society that propagates cartoons that will cradle men from birth to grave while women dominate reality. If a man has a jester-type personality, he needs to take a more concerted effort to limit his consumption of trivialities. He must become "the serious one" in his romantic relationship. Give up the obsessive video game playing and action figure collecting for something that is worth more than both, masculine dignity. When a man starts taking himself seriously is when his woman will start sharing his same thought.

The

wall

is

strong

For a man to display confidence to his woman, he must show her that he is not dependent on frame-crutches. Leadership comes with stress and a successful leader manages his stress successfully. If a man drinks every day, he is showing that his everyday needs a drink. Substance addictions project frame weakness. The reason why many women start building resentment with their men is because their men rely on drugs and alcohol for sanity. That is not a particularly good reassurance of leadership, is it? A man who needs alcohol because he feels like he has a stressful job is man who either needs a new job or a new way to manage his stress. Alcohol is one of the most destructive substances on the planet for masculinity. It dopes up a man's reward center and kills his ambition. When a woman sees her leader binge drinking is a sign that she needs a better leader. And she will plan to find a better man in her heart. Can a man blame a woman for losing faith in his ability to maintain frame if he needs alcohol to do so? Drugs and alcohol are for men who have trouble maintaining the appearance of their frame of realities. These substances are frame crutches and display lack of internal fortitude.

They are easy short cuts to pleasure that rob the spirit of ambitious energies. A man should be careful to limit his consumption and use of drink otherwise he will find himself with years of wasted potential lost behind him. When a man drinks, he will start to experience more shit tests from his woman because of the failure of his masculinity. She cannot help but test his confidence because her leader is losing control over his mind and body.

This creates an anxious and violent environment for women. They increase their shit tests from fear, and this further aggravates the men who are trying to escape their problems. When a man tries to drink his problems away, his problems will increase from the neglect. And just like the expression "When it rains it pours," these men's lives will fill with chaos just as their glass is filled with whiskey.

Drinking only allows a man the temporary relief of problem avoidance. The more a man continues with this lifestyle the more his problems start stacking up until he is forced to address them. This neglect fuels despair because the spirit is overwhelmed from the work required to fix what he allowed to decay. Better to avoid that scenario by either absence or limiting drink to rare occasion. Daily drink is always a problem. It signals that drinking is necessary for a man's daily grind. And when drinking becomes necessary is a signal that a man's frame of reality has become weakened and atrophied. That is why he depends on a frame-crutch.

A man's everyday life should project to himself and to his woman that he believes in his own future. Drugs and alcohol are rituals of disbelief. When a man gets blackout-drunk is a roleplay of non-existence. By holding off drink for tomorrow, a man is telling himself and the world that tomorrow will exist and therefore tomorrow matters. The act of pushing off pleasure is a beautiful symbol of belief.

"But Jerr," a voice calls out from off the page, "Are all drugs and alcohol best to be avoided?"

No. A man can indulge occasionally but only when the indulgence becomes a ritual of moderated strength and not a ritual of surrender to weakness. A man having drinks with friends occasionally is a sign of strength whereas a man drinking alone every night is a sign of decay and disbelief.

A man who can push off pleasure not only displays his inner willpower but strengthens it. For a man to become internally strong, he must push off pleasure. Sound like a chicken and egg scenario? That is because it is. A man builds internal strength by strong external expression. External to internal technique. A man doesn't remain sober because he believes in himself, he remains sober because *he wants to believe in himself.* Daily habits of self-belief are important in building self-belief. Sobriety is rocket fuel for increasing certainty of self. And moderation (if it can be had) is a further reassurance of the certainty of a man's self by his own measured control.

Under

the

shadow

of

the

wall

A woman is merely a reflection of a man. That is why women fundamentally change in relationships dependent on a man's frame. If the man drops masculine frame, the woman will pick it up (bitterly) and when he picks up masculine frame his woman will fall into her feminine frame. A woman's entire being flips dependent on her man's role because a woman's being is dependent on man. A woman is only as stable as the man she is with. When a woman is outside a masculine frame, her reality becomes the sole reality and that existential anxiety leads her to collecting cats and antipsychotics. Without a man's masculine frame, a woman becomes mentally ill. Lesbian relationships are the canary in the coal mine to what happens without a masculine influence. Substance abuse, violence, dead sexuality with crippling anxiety and depression. With the rise of fatherlessness

creating unframed men, we are seeing a
simultaneous rise in women's irrationality.

This effect on our collective conscience is
priming societies for mass hysteria. When a
society becomes feminized, we see elements of
chaos become more abundant. Why? Because
feminine is chaos and when civilization is in its
feminine frame it is in decay. If a man believes in
himself and believes in civilization, then he will
help other men to pick up masculine frame.
When each man picks up frame, their women
will fall into their feminine.

"But Jerr," a voice calls out from outside
the page, "Some of these feminists are really
dominant and hate men... how do we cure
them?"

All women change under the strength of
masculine frame. In the past a woman had to
either obey a man or find another man to obey
otherwise she would be outcast to the wilderness.
That will need to happen for feminism to die
out. But instead of the literal wilderness of the
past it will be in the emotional wilderness of
being outside frame. Without men keeping
feminism alive it would have no other choice but
to fade away. It is men who keep it alive, not
women. Weak men who were tricked into
becoming self-loathing warriors are the ones
keeping it going. We do not need to change
women minds; we need to change our fellow
brothers' minds. Every man that picks up
masculine frame is a man who has joined the
fight against the scourge of feminism. Why?
Because with frame a man changes a woman's
cruelty and dominance to virtue and submission.
Feminism only exists because enough men
abandoned their frames to allow it to exist.
Blame grandpa, not grandma. Women are just a

reflection of weak forefathers who shrugged their burden. When enough men pick up the tools of power is when we will see society flip from feminized to masculinized. The modern world was set up to transfer power from men to women and that is why men are being left behind to suffer in unframed despair.

Does it make any sense to further empower a generation of young women over men when many men do not even have the advantage of masculinity from their fathers? Fatherless men have zero reason to shrug power they were never given. These men have had to suffer without an ounce of privilege and yet they are forced to endure school systems that lift their female peers above them. What men need to realize is that their weak forefathers sold them into slavery. These weak forebears have set up a system where men are being stripped of their pride and authority. This is a desecration of our natural selection and is heinously ignorant of the sexual selection of our species. It will be up to this forgotten generation to correct what our ancestors foolishly unleashed upon the world. It wasn't women who made feminism happen, it was weak men who allowed it to happen. We are in a world of confusion and suffering because of this power shrug. A woman suffers when she has power and so does the man under her authority. They both suffer in sexual confusion. When a man picks up masculine frame and seeks authority in his relationship, he will realize what society is encouraging him to abandon, his sexual dignity. This dignity is rewarded by the woman of our species with respect and sex because she innately knows the necessity of it. Women wouldn't reward a man's masculine frame unless it was needed for survival. Feminism is anti-nature and causes humanity to suffer because of its forced artificiality. It is a lie, and it must be treated as such. Nothing on the planet has caused more masculine humiliation and more feminine sexual dysfunction than feminism. Does a feminist prove to the world that she can satisfy a man in a relationship or is the man under a feminist emasculated? Does the rise of feminism lower birth rates? It is a scourge and a plague on humans. It is the decay in the fabric of civilization and must be viewed as anti-human.

"But Jerr," a voice calls out from off the page, "How do we defeat this false ideology?"

By picking up and carrying masculine frame. By taking authority and by seeking respect for our manhood. A man leads and a woman follows. Let that sink in. *A man leads and a woman follows.* She is but a shadow that is cast out from us. If we take the form she will bend. She moves because we move. That is truth of being a man and the truth of being a woman. We are complements to each other and depend on each other. A woman's complement to a man's authority is a simultaneous complement to her own sexuality. That is why women seek a man with strong leadership qualities, so she can have sexual pleasure. It is in harmony with the biology of our sexual selection.

Modern society speaks of the mind poison of "social construction" only because they want to ignore biology. The world is not one of just social constructs but also of biological certainties. A man leading a woman is a sexual selection certitude.

"But Jerr," a voice calls out from off the page, "I picked up frame. My woman is happily submitting... is that all I need to do to help society and combat feminism?"

A man who only helps himself is a man who doesn't believe in his fellow orphan. It is not good enough to only benefit yourself. The reason I am writing this book is to help men who have been forgotten and neglected like me. If a man wants to help, he can teach other men frame, he can let his friends borrow this book or he can support me and help his friend simultaneously by gifting my book. This message needs to go beyond you alone to have an impact on our society. We must work together to solve this current state of humiliation of mankind. Pick up masculine frame and start handing it out. *Recommend this book.* Men needed this help yesterday.

PICK UP,

CARRY AND

PASS FRAME

The

wall

leads

A man leads a woman around on a date and then consummates with his affection. In a relationship, the man continues to *plan, plot* and *give direction* to his woman. This burden of leadership is picked up from the first moment a man is with a woman until the relationship ends. Unframed men have believed the lie of equality and therefore shrug their leadership. If two people are in a relationship, one will be the leader. There is not a perfectly equal power dynamic in romance. Even lesbians have submissive and dominant roles. If an unframed man is not the leader, then his woman will bear the responsibility with resentment. The feminist lie is that women would want power and not resent it as soon as it is in their hands. The lie is proven by the bitterness formed in a woman when the man becomes weak and shrugs his leadership. *A woman will punish male weakness eternal.* It doesn't matter the newest fads or fashion; a woman will always despise a weak man under her authority in a sexual relationship. A woman in power cannot help but become tyrant over her weak man. She will emasculate him with little pity while depriving him of respect and sex. And that is while fantasizing about stronger men dominating her. These fantasies become real when the woman cheats and abandons her emotionally dependent man. This is the illusion of feminist fairness. *Equality is a lie to transfer power.* A power transfer to resentful hands. Women do not want the power otherwise they would reward men with respect and sex from their elevated position of authority. But when a woman assumes power over a man, she robs him of those two essential elements that men need for their own healthy psychology.

A framed man sets the tone for his leadership early, and it is on the woman to want to follow him or not. If she does not want him for a leader, she will resent his authority with disrespectful behaviors. That is her way of saying that she doesn't love a man and most likely is pining for another. A woman shows her love by respect and sex. When a woman fails at those two, she fails at being in love. And a woman's failure is caused by her man's failure. A man must take responsibility for his own relationship with his woman. He picked her and her disrespect is a response to his weakness. When a man forgets to lead, he is forgetting himself and showing that his mind is elsewhere. He could be wanting to dive into fantasy like an ostrich with its head in the sand. Or he could have lost his confidence from losing his job, hair or becoming sexually impotent. These would all make a man more focused on his self-pity and less focused on dominating his woman. It is a man's duty to dominate and lead his woman. If she is not being led or dominated, then she will seek it somewhere else. Life is cruel that way.

"But Jerr," a voice calls out from off the page, "How does a man go about dominating and leading a woman?"

To dominate a woman, a man needs to be selfish and greedy in his pleasures.

"But Jerr," a voice calls out from off the page, "Isn't greed and selfishness bad... doesn't that prove that he doesn't genuinely love his woman?"

How can a man love something he doesn't understand? When a man takes his greed and selfishness seriously in a relationship, he is reassuring his woman of his confidence. A woman is full of doubt and anxiety, that is why she expects a leader that is confident in his wants and not afraid to pursue them. When a man becomes too agreeable and too giving, what does that project to his woman? That he lacks confidence and isn't sure of himself enough to take what he desires. An unframed man must understand that women fall over themselves to get a chance at greedy and powerful men. These powerful men take what they want. This greedy nature of a framed man is what a woman expects from her boss.

When an unframed man gives a woman everything she wants, this does two things, first it inflates her ego which will cause her to dismiss her current man's leadership and secondly it projects his own fear-of-loss. The more afraid of losing a woman an unframed man is, the more he will try to win her affection with material things. There is nothing more pathetic than an unframed man giving gifts to his unsatisfied woman. This gesture is like pouring gasoline on an already raging fire of dissatisfaction and disbelief. This gift giving for affection and sex demeans a woman to the level of prostitute. It diminishes a woman's perception of her man's self-esteem while diminishing the value of the sex for them both.

"But Jerr," a voice calls out from off the page, "When is it a good time to give gifts to a woman?"

Currency is raised when rarity enforced. If a man wants his gifts to have a positive effect, then he needs to make sure that they are far and few in between. They should project affection not fear-of-loss. When a man is constantly showering his woman with gifts, then he is simultaneously showering her with his fear and anxiety. The measured approach leads a woman to pleasant psychology. A man is restrained and measured in his approach because he wants his approach to have positive value. Unframed men waste their value with overindulgence which backfires on them like pouring water on a grease fire. It does more damage than good.

To be a leader a man must be planning and guiding his woman. This should be a daily process and is reinforced by ritual. It could be as simple as leading her on daily walks or in daily exercise. A man must find a ritual that he wants to lead his woman in. The importance comes not just from the action of his leadership but in the consistency of its execution. Women despise men who start things and quit. Why? Because they see it as feminine and anti-masculine. When a man starts something, he should be disciplined enough to carry through with his plans. Unframed men like to talk about what they are going to do but rarely follow through. Why? Because they receive enough emotional validation from just speech alone which ends up killing their drive for action and results. A framed man holds in his words about his projects because he doesn't want the emotional validation that would give him the reward hit-in his brain that would kill his ambition. When a woman sees a man start a project, he should finish it for his own reputation's sake. He needs to build a reputation of "If I say it will happen, it happens." This will inflate the currency of his words and build his woman's faith in his leadership. A man being "a man of his word" is truth. Without the authority of speech, a man becomes like a jester and less like a king. Using less words increases that value and so does follow-through. To have the king's speech is built brick by brick with a man's measured discipline. The reason why a woman will respect a framed man's words is because he has worked his ass off to secure that reputation, just like everything else in his life. It takes willpower and enough work ethic to follow through on what was started.

A man who leads his woman in daily ritual understands the importance of training her perception. If a man fails to lead his woman but gets upset when she is forced to lead him is a man who creates his own problem. These men will complain about women even though they are to blame. Take leadership. It will not be given to you by her. A man must make the plan and lead her through it. This is good for the relationship and she will prove it to him by rewarding him with respect and sex. Those two are how a man knows he is fulfilling his role correctly. The woman rewards what the man should be doing and punishes the man for failure to do what he should be doing. This is the nature of the sexual selection of our species. A woman directs it with respect and sex. Respect and sex are what motivates men to be better men. This is the gift for all the hard work of carrying frame.

Unframed men fail in leadership because they prefer the emotional dependency of friendship with their women. A romantic relationship is not about friendship, it is about sex. A man who wants to be friends with his woman is a man who wants to shrug his leadership. A man is a leader with his woman, not her friend. That is what her girlfriends are for. She needs to have a woman she is best friends with, and the man needs a man to be friends with or at least he needs to be secure enough with his own company. The issue with modern romance is men end up burdening their women with roles beyond sexual partner. Men want someone that will reassure them emotionally. This commonality with men is because too many men are emotionally weak. If they were emotionally strong, then they would not expect their women to be friends or even worse, a mother figure. She is a romantic partner and a follower. Do not try to force her into more responsibilities than she wants. That is why a woman will punish a man time and time again when the man starts to depend on the woman for emotional support. She needs a masculine man for her own emotional needs. She needs a rock to steady the waves of her emotional chaos, not a man who is in the same internal turmoil as she is. Be her amused stone and lead her to shared victory.

Plot, plan and guide. That is what a man needs to do daily, week, monthly and yearly in his relationship. This solidifies his role as leader and calms his woman's anxiety and fear.

The

wall

does

not

apologize

or

explain

There is a John Wayne quote, "Never apologize, Mister, it's a sign of weakness." And the Duke speaks masculine truth. When a man apologizes to his woman, he does a tremendous frame break. It is the most validation seeking behavior there is on the planet. Seeking forgiveness shows weakness of internal frame as it places a woman above in an authoritarian position like a judge. She sits on a throne and deems a man absolved from his badness. That is what a man does when he apologizes to a woman, he places her in authority over him. Do not be surprised if the ego-inflated woman becomes cruel in her position of authority. When a man says "sorry" he bends his knee emotionally before his woman. And when men bend the knee to their women, they get the axe. A man who apologizes to a woman is like a child tugging on her skirt and telling her he needs a diaper change. That is the revulsion a woman feels when her man makes himself weak before her. And if the woman's revulsion has become normalized, she will be in reptilian-exploitation-mode. A woman does not have the capacity to feel pity over an unframed man. When a man makes it known that he is weak, he becomes like a slave offering himself up for slavery. Should the slave trader feel guilty putting the shackles on or will she just snap them on in her gained opportunity?

Apologies are dangerous tactics in the battlefield of romance.

"But Jerr," a voice calls out from off the page, "Shouldn't a man apologize sometimes?"

On rare occasion a man must apologize. But only because he is ashamed of his lack of masculinity before his woman. For example, if a man loses his temper and becomes emotional, then he should apologize to show that he is ashamed over his behavior. That should be rare as a man with masculine frame shouldn't lose his temper that often. Otherwise, a man should just let things be. He should use words like "regret", "failure" and "mistake" but never "sorry." That word is repulsive to a woman when the man saying it is framed. They do not want to see their big, bold, fearless leader sullying his tongue with such a pathetic word. It is pollution to the needed trust in a man's leadership. Apologies should best be avoided because it projects doubt of a man's own internal frame of reality. When a man is a confessor-type, he will carry more internal doubt which causes him to rely on a woman for emotional and moral validation. He

238

will see her as his moral judge which will compel him to apologize for her validation. A woman doesn't want a man that is reliant on her emotionally. That is disgusting to her. It repulses women when a man is emotionally weak and cannot manage his own conscience. This repulsion leads to resentment and distrust in authority.

Sometimes an apology is necessary, but it should be just as rare as a man's tears.

Another sign of weakness is when a man overly explains himself.

"But Jerr," a voice calls out from outside the page, "How are explanations a sign of weakness?"

Because to explain is to feel an explanation is needed and an explanation is only needed when there is doubt in authority. It continues a frame of doubt. I am not meaning that all explanation is wrong only that *the more a man explains himself, the more he doubts himself.* A woman needs to be in "trust her man's words" mode. If she questions her man's authority then she does not respect her man's authority. When a man questions himself and overly explains himself, he becomes like a nervous crook before a cop. The more explanation needed, the greater the projection of doubt and need for lying. Trust should be the assumption unless confusion is admitted. When a man starts believing in himself, he will start valuing his own words and not killing that currency with doubtful over explanations. Over explanation is like saying "Trust me, trust me, trust me" which only elicits distrust. Nobody believes words less than a woman. Words to a woman are based on emotion and emotions are always true which makes them also always false. This emotional reasoning makes a woman's words true even when she's lying. That is why women distrust women. That is why a man should be "a man of his word." Because to have authority over a woman in a relationship, a man's speech must be trusted. She puts her trust in the anti-feminine. It is the lack of explanation over a man's words that builds her confidence.

An unframed man will lack belief in himself to such a high degree that he will use other authority placeholders for his own authority. For example, "[another important guy] says", in the woman's mind she will say, "Well as long as you didn't say it and it came from a reputable source." A man who places another man above himself in authority within his romantic relationship is always pathetic to the woman. When a man is talking to his woman he should just speak plain and let his own words carry authority. No need for him to cite sources or to lift another man above himself in authority. It all takes time and effort to overcome this deep lack of self-belief. Many unframed men who were raised by single mothers have absorbed this feminine self-doubt over their speech and end up moralizing it to spare their ego. Most weak things an unframed man thinks are not equated in his mind with weakness but rather "humility." Unframed men protect their decisioning with false morality. They dig their own psychological graves. Every shovelful of weak action has a shovelful of false morality behind it. And they keep digging and digging until they wonder why they allowed themselves to get to that point of deep humiliation. It is because they hid behind their self-perceived morality and were not truthful with themselves. Why? Because the truth requires a man to acknowledge that his personality may be incorrect which hurts his vanity. Also, it requires him to admit that he has spent a lifetime of ego investment in something that was foolish. The truth requires work and effort in changing self-made failure. Killing a personality is a bitch. We all love our own personalities and to admit that we built it wrong takes deep humility.

True humility is admitting that a man has had false humility. When an unframed man admits that he has apologized and over explained himself from weakness and not humility is when he will be able to show the truth of himself. This pride in a man will be rewarded by his woman by her increasing her respect for his authority.

The

wall

absorbs

blame

Nothing gives more relief to a woman than a man willing to bear her responsibility. Women are like children who want to play while father worries. That is why when a man picks up masculine frame, a woman will fall into her feminine. This allows her to exist in a more irresponsible mode than if she were with an unframed man. No creature on the planet is more Darwinian than a woman. She exists purely in survival mode and will easily trample a man to free herself of burden. That is why a woman becomes something she doesn't recognize when paired with an unframed man. She picks up his frame and hits him over the head with it. And if she cheats on the poor sap, he will get the blame. All blame flows back to man. Why? Because all things are dependent on man, not woman. *To be a man is to bear the responsibility of all things.* And that includes women. What an unframed man must realize is that no matter how much he tries to share responsibility with a woman, she will still place all blame on him if and when things fall apart. And things always fall apart. There is nothing more typical than a woman after making a mistake needing to share blame. A woman will use all ten fingers to point to ten different people for her own failure. Placing and sharing blame is feminine nature. When a framed man fails, even if people under him contributed to the failure, he will assume responsibility for them all. That is what a leader does, he takes blame.

Why do women innately shrug accountability? Because they are collective minded and have a greater fear of social demonization. They fear being outcasts to the group that they depend on for emotional validation. When they are outcasted from their group they cease to emotionally exist. And so, they cannot help but lie and throw blame off themselves in order to preserve their essential reputation within their collective. To be outside the collective is to die in their ancestral memory. That is why women will blame others and especially blame men for their mistakes. This responsibility shrug is an animal response for self-preservation. What always shocks an unframed man is when he is blamed after a relationship falls apart. How can a woman blame him when he purposely shared responsibility down the line throughout the relationship? This part of feminine nature is total confusion to unframed men since they were indoctrinated with an egalitarian mindset. When a woman speaks of an abusive ex-boyfriend, a framed man knows she is throwing blame on him to preserve her own virtue. No other time in a man's life will he be villainized and demonized more so than when a romantic relationship falls apart. Framed men know this because framed men are wise to feminine nature. They assume responsibility over all things in the relationship and they expect their women to be irrational in blaming their character when things don't work out. Women rely on reputation destruction because it is the most meaningful attack they have. When a being is unframed emotionally, they will be able to spin whatever narrative they want inside their heads and make it true. If it feels true, it must be true, is how they emotionally rationalize. That is why framed men do not put much stock in women's words. Their word does not have the same meaning and currency as a man who exists above emotion. When a man lies, he knows he is lying. But when a woman lies, she makes herself believe the lie before selling it.

If any man is reading this and encounters a woman in romance who speaks ill of a previous boyfriend, just be aware of how a woman operates before you buy into her narrative.

When a boy is raised by a single mother, many times he will be told a devil's story about his father. Many women unfortunately sour their children's minds from their own embittered spirit. This increases the self-loathing within fatherless boys who will demonize their own gender based on the mother's version of events. Being without a father is hard enough without also associating all men with devils. This twisted spirit harms a young boy long into adulthood as he must untwist the mother's narrative himself and redeem his manhood. When a man understands the truth about his own nature, as well as women, he will realize that women are not more moral beings than men. They are corrupt and foolish. But by altering expectations, a man can enjoy a relationship with a woman as long as he doesn't expect absolute truth to pour out of her mouth.

When a woman cheats on a man she will not only hurt the man by her treachery, but she will also increase his self-hatred by gaslighting him into believing his supposed villainy was the ultimate cause in order to relieve herself of all culpability. A woman cannot handle her own failure and so she will drag a man's reputation through mud in order to make herself feel clean. This is her animal nature and must be expected. Just as a lion roars, a woman will place blame away from herself. Do not place weight upon a woman's speech. Do not be consumed by her shame and guilt tactics. This is her way to save face and how she controls emotionally weak men. We are not controlled by siren songs of emotion that lead us astray. We know how the lion roars and we will not surrender to the noise.

The

wall

investigates

By now, you will understand two major points of feminine nature. A woman wants to use her intuition to unpack a mystery and she expects a man to act like a woman in the same sense to unpack her mystery. That is why when a woman betrays a man and the man is confused, the woman will say "The *signs* were there."

"What signs?" The man will scratch his head in heartbreak. Do you see what the woman expects from a man? She expects him to be just as intuitive as she is. She expects him to unpack subtle clues and to pay attention to small indicators of communication. A woman expects a man to be a woman. Women do not realize that men attempt to communicate with as much clarity as possible. And that masculine speech is built to kill any mystery in order to simplify meaning. Men speak plain to avoid confusion. Women speak in signs to incite imagination. They feed on the mystery of emotion which allows them ego expansion while protecting the egos of others from emotional pain. This imaginary and ego driven style of speaking prompts women to interrupt each other frequently from intuitive presumption. That is why women have more complex communication styles than men. Subterfuge incites imagination while protecting hurt feelings. They use language to expand their own ego while condescending to the sensitivity of others. This dual motive is why they remain subtle in communication. That is why in a feminized environment language becomes watered down and confused. It encourages use of intuition to spare feelings. Political correctness is feminine speech that follows this complex sensitive framework. Politically correct speech is an attack on masculine speech. Women will build the most elaborate speech system to avoid addressing the elephant in the room. They speak in riddles and in shadows. A man speaks plain and cuts through complexity with his own simplicity. A feminized environment will communicate with verbal redirection such as irony, sarcasm and understatement that requires subtle clues of facial expression. Shadow speak comes from a state of passive aggression and is feminine in nature. Hidden language is necessary for emotional beings who become easily traumatized by direct communication. Why? Because direct communication is hurtful to the sensitive who depend on emotional validation from others for their own existence. It comes from a collectivist spirit as a feminized being will feel high anxiety if outcast from her group. Women have depended on groups for survival since the beginning and that is why they are controlled by groupthink. That is why in our feminist times we see more speech control to protect others from "harm." That is why in our feminist times we see "safe spaces" being created to protect the sensitive from ear trauma. *Speaking plain is violence to feminists.* They will not stop until every masculine tongue is removed from every living man to protect their feminine ears.

It is important for a man to understand this because a woman will expect it from him. Why? Because *to be a man is to bear the responsibility of all things.* It is not good enough for a man to understand his own masculinity, he must understand feminine nature just as a fisherman understands his fishing equipment and the fish he seeks. A man must understand two worlds to be in authority over them both. A man understands that a woman will expect him to be a detective to her clues of emotion. That is why a man must be aware of the changes in his woman's behavior and whether she is sending subtle signs that she is up to no good. Remember, a woman will never take responsibility for her actions. She will expect the man to prevent her from flirting with disaster. She will act devious in secret and then blame the man for not preventing the covert act. That is how women operate and it will not change until the end of our species. They are hidden by nature but still demand to be seen. They need a man to watch them as if they were a child playing by a street. A man must pick up on deviations and apply strict rules over his woman. *There is no authority without rules.* Is she getting dressed up a lot and going out with the girls? Most likely she is advertising her body for possible sexual opportunity. Did you let her do it? Too bad, she will cheat and still blame you. That is how life works for a man. Speak plain to her "I don't like you going out dressed sexy. If you do, we are done."

See that? *That is balls.* If she loves you, she will not only obey but she will be turned on. That is how female nature works. They are aroused by masculine authority. Keep tabs on her and investigate her sexual behavior. Women cannot help but sexualize themselves to other men, that is why they need strong men to make them obey. Do not be violent. Framed men use fear of loss to establish rules. "My way or the highway" is the only power we truly have. And women understand that a man must have authority for the relationship to succeed. Investigate and do not be afraid to cut through her subtle signs with direct speech. And do not be afraid to harm her sensitive ears with plain speak.

249

The

wall

deflects

shame

Women are obsessed with speech control because they have relied on speech as their sole means of control over men for millennia. A man could be the size of King Kong but if he is emotionally weak then he can be controlled with only small movements from a feminine tongue. *Guilt and shame tactics are feminine in nature.* They will shame and guilt a man until the man begs for redemption. And a woman who sets herself up as redeemer to a man, assumes authority over him. That is why women encourage men to be emotional, so that their words will have a greater impact for control. If a man is more rational than emotional, shame labels do little to affect his internal reality. Why? Because he doesn't rely blindly on group validation for his own peace of mind. He doesn't rely on his woman's judgment of his character for the easing of his conscience. When a society becomes feminized, it becomes sensitive to shame. That is why women encourage coddling younger generations into safe spaces. It is how they gain power over a groomed generation of men who can be easily influenced by guilt tactics. One tactic that women will use to control, is to use the word "science" as a personage to control others. For example, if a there is a collectivist politic that is agreed upon by a group of scientists, a woman will say "Science says" or "Let the science speak." They use a powerful word like "science" to make weak-willed men submit. Do these women understand the science? Can they cite the scientist names and the research papers? No. What they are doing is saying "Listen to the holy priesthood on the hill that agrees with me." Are scientists an uncorrupted group with only pure interests as if they are a holy priesthood? No. They are men just like you and me. They are men who accept bribes, they are men controlled by ego and they are men controlled by politic. And they are men who disagree with each other. There is nothing more simple-minded than shaming others by saying "SCIENCE!" as if the word itself should make someone drop to their knees in reverence. The word itself has replaced God to some. In the past it was "God says" but now it is "Science says." Do not bend the knee to feminists who try to shame you into obedience to some men who most likely were funded by a few globalist elites.

Or feminists will try to shame men into believing the mainstream media's propaganda. They will use newspapers as holy texts of belief. "Look at what the experts say" they will showcase the printed word to back up the preconceived belief system. But what they fail to see is that journalists have become activists and that the mainstream media is nothing more than a blatant mouthpiece for left-wing propaganda. *To be a real journalist is to print something that disagrees with your worldview.* These media activists would never do that because they are zealots for their political mission. And just like over-protective mother hens, they do not trust the masses with free information. They perceive the masses in condescension as imbeciles who would fumble the truth in their hands.

That is not the only shame label feminine beings use. Women also overuse the word "racist" to make men submit. Men in the past would use the word sparingly to single out extreme cases, but what does a woman do? She overuses the word to such a degree that it becomes watered down to nothing. When a being is emotionally charged and unframed, she will overuse words that most encapsulate her singular negative emotion. She will cry wolf to such a degree that all meaning becomes lost. *That is why women inflate not the currency of a word but the emotion of the individual in hearing a word.* Women innately know they collapse words, that is why they heighten sensitivity overall to the overused speech.

Emotional beings are unbounded and cannot help but be pulled along uncontrolled. That is why women represent chaos and disorder. When they assume total control over something it crumbles under their power, just as *words collapse under their control.* For example, "racist" used to mean someone that expressed hate towards someone of a different race based on race. But radicalized feminists in modern times have deemed all whites as "racist," even the ones who were raised to see beyond race. *When something becomes everything, it becomes nothing.* During the last fifty years racism has decreased in the United States and yet feminists believe it is increasing. *Racism decreased but emotions increased.* For the past fifty years, forgotten generations of children have been raised outside rational male frames. They have been raised with only their mothers' feminine frame of emotion and have absorbed their feminine sense of oppression. These single mothers blamed the world and taught their children to do the same. They continued not the tradition of self-responsibility but passed their irrational self-victimization onto them. The feeling of racism increased, not the reality. Interior emotions deceive the mind from exterior realities.

This emotionally irrational use of language will increase more racism in the world not less. Why? Because this false labeling will group decent white folk with Klansman. See the madness? What is a Klansman, a bad "racist"? We must protect decent people from being slurred as evil before they surrender to the label like children who are told they are bad and so they fulfill their own demonization. Women's innate sense of intuition drives them to a place of obscure understanding. From their high neuroticism outside masculine frame, they fall into tilting at windmills. They metaphorically wash their hands yet still feel unclean and so they wash and wash until their skin falls off. And they expect others to understand their circular logic with its many rabbit holes. Instead of creating a new word to express themselves, they watered down an existing (and useful word) to pointlessness. The word "racism" itself *collapsed* under radical feminist control.

When men pick up masculine frame with rationality, they cannot be controlled by guilt manipulation. A woman can call them a "[blank]-phobe" of any kind and it will not have an effect. Especially in a highly feminized environment where women shame men for every little thing. The more they shame, the less the shaming works. That is, if men become less emotional in nature and see women's tactics as neurotic manipulations. Feminist shaming will fall apart from the sheer anality of it. *All neuroticism is feminine.* And when enough women exist outside masculine frame, neuroticism skyrockets in society. That is why new shame labels are being created every day along with new identity labels. Madness is running rampant because the tradition of frame which is a check to the power of womankind has been abandoned. Just twenty years ago the word "racist" conjured in the mind images of a person burning crosses in a black person's yard to terrorize them. But now feminists want all whites to be considered the same as what I just described. And it doesn't end with race. Just twenty years ago alternative sexuality was considered LGBT but now there are sixty-four different identities and climbing. So, they added an unlimited "+" at the end. And each new sexual identity label comes with a special label of "-phobe" to shame men into accepting the madness. Society is crumbing from this insanity because women's neuroticism is not being controlled by strong masculine frames.

Feminists will try to shame me for writing this book by labeling me a "sexist." Am I a sexist? First, what is a sexist? To me being pro men makes me a proud man and a realist to how necessary masculinity is for women's mental health. Does it make a woman sexist if she believes her way is better than a man's way? No. She is wrong, but it doesn't make her a sexist. Everyone believes their way is superior. If a man is sexually harassing and humiliating a woman in a workplace, to me, he is sexist. Which I would not agree with. The term "sexist" should be used in rarity for ultimate impact. Not watered down to a degree where the word itself collapses. I do not want to live in a society where it is okay to sexually harass women. Why? Because I have deep love for my mother and sisters and want to protect them. But that doesn't mean just because I love the women in my family that I will shrug my masculine pride and authority. Every woman in my family should be under a masculine frame.

A man's masculine frame is not tyrannous and violent like a feminine frame. Every woman deserves the peace that comes from being under a man's benign and strong frame. That is the society that I believe in.

The

wall

competes

There is an old song that my sisters loved that I remember hearing growing up. It was called "Anything you can do (I can do better)" from the musical *Annie Get Your Gun*. This song was about a competitive woman wanting to beat a man she had romantic attraction to in various activities. The song is a bit silly, but it captures the psychology of romantic friction perfectly. A woman is always reaching for the crown and a man must deny her for both their arousal. It is a man's supreme confidence and competence that a woman most desires. She desires to fight like hell for supremacy only to lose to a greater beast. When a man loses, both lose out sexually but when a man wins, both win sexually. A man must always win in competition against his woman. This reassures them both, playfully, of his necessity for leadership. When a woman wins, it signals a failure of that necessity. Even in games the subconscious is triggered.

"But Jerr," a voice calls out from off the page, "My woman always beats me in games... what am I to do?"

Pick a game where you can beat her and only choose that game to play. If you do lose in a game, use charisma to shield the failure. But a man should always pick what he is best at for competition. A woman will not admit it, but she wants to be conquered by her man in competition. That is why this current participation trophy generation of men need to take beating girls seriously. Competition is masculine in spirit. Men sharpen men in competition, and we conquer women in competition. Losing a game is not the biggest deal in the reality of all things but a man should always seek victory over a woman. This winning spirit is what women expect from their men. They do not want men who lack the spirit of competition. They want the fire in the blood that only masculine men have. We look at everything as winners and losers. Everything, even if in fun.

The

wall

is

civilized

The rise of fatherlessness has created a world that is ruled by emotion over rationality. Weak men allowed the government to subsidize single motherhood which has increased emotionalism throughout the world. It was generations of weak men who allowed this feminine frame to propagate and spread. Weak politicians, weak religious leaders and weak men ruled by sex who allowed this power transfer to happen under their noses. They let the flood of chaos pour out from womankind and wash away all common sense.

With total control of modern psychology of our forgotten generation having been in woman's hands we have seen the spread of madness and despair. This emotionalism that our mothers taught us has made our minds reactive and primitive. No longer do we have the father's rational mind influencing our lives.

The laws in western civilization have favored womankind at the expense of boys' need for fatherly direction. *The government has given mothers total control over our present reality.* And how does it look? Does it look like decay and madness? Is sexual chaos rising? Are we

seeing a rise in identity crisis among the youth?
Are institutions collapsing?

We now live inside a world controlled by
unbounded feminine nature. Civilization is not in
decline; it is in free fall. The modern mind has
become primitive in its emotional decay. This
primitive state is accelerating at a rapid pace
under feminist control. And at this speed of
devolution, we will again see something like
Neanderthals rise among our communities. We
will see nothing but unframed madness because
of the arrogance of deeming men obsolete in
raising children. Why didn't anyone think about
what would happen to a society if they only had
feminine influence on a generation of children?
Wasn't that a mistake of massive proportion?
The future unframed state of mankind if it
continues can be likened to when one infant
starts to cry which triggers a room full of babies
to start crying. If each frame is emotional and
reactionary then we could expect a domino effect
of insanity. Mass hysteria will lead to collapse of
systems and networks because individuals have
been primed to be emotionally reactive. *This
mass unframing cataclysm will create an instant
primitivism which will turn man to animal.* The
world is being primed for emotional breakdown
by abandoning masculinity.

That is why it is crucial to deem
masculine frame essential to the psychology of
growing children by law and begin passing out
frame in every society immediately. We must
pass frame because it is never too late to frame
the fatherless. I was able to frame myself and
overcome the feminine frame of authority in my
mind. That is my hope in writing this book is to
civilize our mankind away from the primitive
state of female nature. We must go forward in

our civilization and not slip back to our
primordial past.

260

Crumbling

walls

around

us

Decay breeds decay. With the rise of
faithlessness more and more men are adopting
the mother's victim complex as part of their ego
defense. They see the world through the lens of
those that bear responsibility, who can be blamed
for problems and themselves who are too weak
to bear the load of existence.

When a man confronts reality and what is
expected of him, he can either summon the
strength to face life or he can find an excuse for
running away. The cowardice is too much to bear
for his ego, so he will construct a story to protect
his reputation.

That is the allure of the Peter Pan
syndrome. We have less mentally ill people in
the world than we think. We have people
running from problems and hiding under
blankets. They know that the mentally ill are not
expected to bear responsibility and so they
celebrate their own psychologically impaired
condition.

From this state of cowardice, they blink
before their bathroom mirror, godless and full of
Darwinist hedonism and see nothing but the

abyss of their animal state. Instead of transcending the human condition, they shiver in the cave of their life and become full of despair. This anxiety and fear overwhelm them to such a degree that the mental illness story becomes realized from its initial cowardice to self-made reality. They believe it until it becomes true inside them just like a woman's "emotional truth."

How do these men relieve their existential anxiety? By identifying with the harmless and irresponsible. They hide among children's toys in order to protect their ego from the sanity that is required of them.

We see in modern times more men diving into fantasy because they fear reality. The overwhelming reality that hangs over their head is like a hideous monster that scares them under their security blankets. They indulge in infantilization to further identify away from what is expected of them. They obsess over Anime and children's cartoons to relieve this anxiety of life. Otto Rank said, "The adult may have fear of death or fear of sex, the child has a fear of life itself."

How do these men rationalize their existence? By hiding behind the victim complex. They externalize all their problems away from themselves and blame everyone for their own self-created problems. Mental illness must be treated not celebrated.

In a feminized society the cult of victimization grows strong. Why? Think about it this way. Self-victimization does two things in an emotional environment. It allows the individual to shrug responsibility while attracting positive attention from the surrounding emotional group.

That is why women and feminized men will take pride in their self-victimization. They showcase victimhood in pride for positive attention and to avoid negative attention. Nothing gives feminized beings more anxiety than negative social attention. But if they had a magic card to play to avoid that social heat then their need for positive emotional validation would be protected from criticism. That is why in modern times we will see more men and women celebrating their mental illnesses as badges of honor to escape responsibility.

The problem grows larger when these individuals find not help but support groups to ease their conscience. By sharing insanity, they normalize the guilt over their shrug of responsibility which allows them to fetishize it as roleplay. They hold conventions to reaffirm themselves as not broken but eternal. They view themselves as brave instead of immature. They have flipped their initial coward response to brave oddity. This irrationality is from their feminine unframed state. It is an irrational loop that will fuel their neurotic state until it culminates to a nervous breakdown which will collapse their reality. If they are wise and have masculine frames guiding them from the loop, the breakdown can be a breakthrough into a new beginning.

These celebrants of infancy fear the deep end of the pool of life and so they splash in the kiddie pool. But instead of being ashamed from their cowardice they deem it brave to be seen in such a humiliated way. These men identify with children to such a degree that soon they view themselves as children like a former moonwalker once did. They do not view themselves as pedophiles since they see themselves as children.

The same could be said of men who dress up as animals. These men do not see themselves as being playful with bestiality since they are roleplaying themselves as beasts. This warped psychology is spreading more and more in our fatherless society. These men must be pulled from their sick fantasies into the burden of adulthood and the sanity that is required of it.

The danger of this psychology beyond where the sexuality can lead to is that the totems of possession will eventually turn to ash leaving these men in a hell state. For example, when a young child is playing with a toy, he cannot imagine himself being at an age where the toy would be meaningless. But we all transcend the child state to the adult state eventually. And when a man's frame-crutch is a cartoon, video game or toy only sets him up for further trauma when those magical objects deaden in their glow and can no longer be enjoyed. The loss of the adolescent comforts further spirals these individuals into the dark abyss of identity crisis and despair.

"But Jerr," a voice calls out from outside the page, "My whole life is based around Anime and video games... what am I to do?"

Confront reality. Do something as simple as watching the evening news. Look upon the trauma of reality and do not look away. This can train a man in becoming strong in dealing with reality. The water may be frigid but after the initial shock the skin becomes desensitized. Cold water is a harsh reality just as images of war are a harsh reality. Do not depend on cartoons produced for children to ease the anxiety of existence. This behavior is just as bad as a drug addict who depends on a drug to manage the normal stress of his life. It only spirals into more dependence and desperation. Every man deserves the sanity of masculine frame. Be strong and turn away from childhood and do not look back. Turn away from the digital castration that leads to madness. Turn away from what is cute and face what is difficult. Turn away from the illusions that pacify. Drop the toys before they turn to ash in your hands. Leave it behind as we expand into the future of our dignified manhood.

265

The

wall

is

sound

A woman cannot afford to have her man become emotionally dependent on her. His frame is the walled garden that protects her from her own emotional chaos. The protector role of a man goes beyond just making sure a woman is physically safe and extends to easing-the-suffering of her own self-doubt. She needs a framed man to help her deal with the level of anxiety that is innate to a woman's existence. If a man has anxiety problems, he will inflame his woman's inherent anxiety and doubt. Why do you think a woman craves a strong man's certitude? It is because his certitude is a complement to her doubt. If a man is doubtful then his woman will have to be the certain one while dealing with her own emotional issues. Sound tough? It is and that is why women become embittered by the experience. A man who depends on his woman for emotional support is cruelly punishing her sensitive nature. She needs a rock, not a wet blanket.

"But Jerr," a voice calls out from off the page, "I have anxiety and depression... does that mean I shouldn't talk about either with my woman?"

Anxiety and depression are both failures of masculinity. If a man shares his negative emotions with his woman, it reveals that he cannot handle his own reality. Do not allow yourself to depend on your woman. That is not what a sexual relationship is for. She is your woman, and she needs you to be strong. Don't like it? Then go ahead risk losing her. It is your own choice. A man must live with the choices he makes in life. But just realize the level of selfishness that is required to depend emotionally on an emotional being. We are men, we do not need emotional dependency. We handle our emotions and psychological issues with rationality and exercise. We use the external-to-internal technique for resolving internal turmoil. We discipline the body until our insides match in order.

When a man deals with madness, his woman will abandon him. It is the same if a man loses his job, he risks losing his woman. She needs a man to save her from reality and not one who drags her down. That is the cruelty of life and that is why a man must seek as much respect and sex as he can. We earn every goddamn thing we want in a relationship. The cruel fate of being a man is that we must bear the reality of all things, even our own punishment. A woman leaves an anxious man because she is escaping an aura of trauma to her spirit. She truly must escape for her own sanity and wellbeing.

It is a man's responsibility to bear his own madness. He cannot share what he fears because he must lead the woman through the brutal reality of existence. A woman may not articulate it but her natural state is between existential anxiety and existential terror. Her normal psyche floats on the despair and elation of the emotional human experience. If a man fails to provide for or protect his woman, she will be thrown into existential terror which causes her to take-to-flight. Her truest belief is in saving her own skin. This ancestral memory comes from women being dependent on men for survival while they carried children in the womb. If the man is "dying," the woman knows to flee to continue the genetic memory. It might sound cruel, but it is how we exist and how we've been able to survive as a species.

Inside her mind is an algorithm that runs based on pure reflex "Flee if protector/provider fails."

When a man understands his expendability, he can start expecting more from his life. Why? Because it is rough being a man and when we fulfill our roles, we deserve reward for our effort. There are many unframed men who gave their women everything they wanted, and the women still left when things got bad. A man doesn't stay with a woman because he believes she will be loyal eternal; he stays because he enjoys her company. *Do not overthink the permanence of things.* There is not a bigger illusion than expecting stability from reality. A framed man does not expect his woman to be stable, but he does expect himself to be stable for her. This is the burden of masculinity and sexual dynamics. Being a leader comes with high reward and high punishment.

"But Jerr," a voice calls out from off the page, "Reward? All I get is punished by women..."

That is why I wrote this book. Men have a difficult time in our sexual selection and need to start expecting more from women. A framed man's responsibility within a relationship can feel heavy at first when a man is starting to pick up frame, but the reward eases the suffering of the burden. When a man starts getting the respect and sex that he desires, it will help in his motivation for carrying his masculine frame. When a woman is with a man with a wall, she will happily throw gifts over the top to show her appreciation. A man who picks up frame will begin to notice behavioral changes in his woman to being more submissive after he practices it for a while. That should be enough motivation for bearing the load of masculinity.

To deal with anxiety a man must take time to exercise and correct his diet. Sometimes an anxiety problem is related to a man having a leaky gut.

When a man's body is not taken care of properly, his mind will rebel against him. If a man applies the external-to-internal technique of exercise, this can ease his worry and despair. Personally, I have at times felt the darkest valley of trouble in my mind that seemed completely rational and real. But after cutting out booze and starting a schedule of running, the "completely-rational" despair evaporated from my thoughts. That is why it is immensely important not to believe the doubter within yourself and to shake off the negative feelings with self-care.

The

wall

and

politic

We live in an age where women have forsaken God and family for state worship. These women without faith and children are detached from the natural order of biology and have become pure political animals. All feminism is political and *radical feminism is rising.* To these women going to the voting booth is just as sacred as going to church was for their grandmas. They increase the size of government just as ancient pagans increased the size of their stone gods. If the god becomes bigger, then its salvation would feel surer. That is why a woman will solve all societal issues by giving power to governmental authority. The government has become her savior. Instead of self-reliance, women will throw all their belief in government hands solving their problems. And where does that leave men? When the authority of government increases, the sovereignty of the individual decreases. How? Take for example if all healthcare becomes controlled by government. How would that affect the individual? His lifestyle would be scrutinized along with his diet. The freedom of choice would be taken away from him. Why? Because by giving government authority over health requires them to take authority over their patient's life. Certain food would be outlawed. There would be mandatory tests that a person would be *forced* to take. There would be mandatory vaccines that an individual would be *forced* to take. The individual must sacrifice his sovereignty to the gods of government authority. Remember, nothing is free. If the government gives with one hand it takes with the other. The more power to government, the less power to people. Do women care? No. They prefer safety over freedom. They would rather give up their individual liberty for safe dependency. But what they fail to realize is that once government attains supreme power over people, these people become nothing but faceless cogs in the machine. Instead of citizens being motivated by their own monetary gain, they would be motivated by gun point. And an individual's belief itself would become blaspheme to the state. To feed the poor requires jailing the religious. Why? Because when all authority is given to the state it will require loyal worship. There can be no gods but one before its throne. And the best way to focus worship is through a cult of personality. Authoritarian states erect statues and direct all belief through the image of one man. That is why totalitarian states outlaw religion. The state is a jealous god.

Do women know this? Most likely not. And would they care? Most likely not. Why? Because most feminists have been indoctrinated in atheism already. They have already been groomed for state worship. It will be the ultimate destination of radical feminism. In that environment masculinity itself will be outlawed as any *individual* will be considered enemy to the hive mind.

A framed man prides himself on his self-reliance and individualism. That is why a man should be wary of anything free from government. That is why framed men fight for smaller government. "Less government" is the masculine creed. Think about power like a weighted scale. The bigger the government, the smaller the individual must be. The bigger the individual, the smaller the government must be. And whether it is left or right wing, both sides can fall into excessive government growth and authoritarianism. The only difference is left-wing ideology which is based on "give a man a fish" instead of "teach a man to fish" expands governmental power by offering free services by design. That is why women and feminists tend to be left-wing. They allow their emotions and bleeding hearts to carry them to self-appointed slavery. A man would rather be free on a pile of dirt than be a slave to government "luxury." Do not rely on government unless you are willing to surrender your soul. And always make sure as much power as possible is in your individual hands.

272

The

wall

is

the

revolution

We live in a feminist establishment because generations of weak men dropped frame which caused them to lose power in their relationships and over their children. We live in a feminist establishment because women are collectivist and gain power through their coordinated voting bloc. We live in a feminist establishment because fathers have been disempowered by governments who have robbed them of authority over their children by giving women total psychological control over their upbringing. We live in a feminist establishment because our societies have become promiscuous which has created a large group of both celibates and eternal bachelors who have little positive influence over the women in their society. These sexless and oversexed men had little authority over the political mind of womankind because women had to exist outside their frames. This environment created single mothers who had total power of conditioning over the young minds of multiple generations of children in our society. These children grew up with a feminine frame of authority in their minds and have based their lives on protecting the mother's way. No other two things have disempowered men more than the welfare state and the celebration of promiscuousness. The father's way has been forgotten because fathers have been forgotten. For change to happen, men must empower themselves and protect their own interests. Men must lift their needs above women and fight like hell for their fellow man.

A hundred years of feminism has dissolved the family into ruin. The laws that protect women in every country only emboldens their cruelties. Governments and weak politicians are to blame for pushing men down into submission. School systems are to blame for indoctrinating men into believing that by giving up power to women they are somehow heroic. These young minds are being poisoned into fetishizing their own subjection. But what these young minds do not realize is that women are already on top and men are below them in the power structure of modern society. Do not think just because a few men are in power at the tip top that a patriarchy exists. Most of western civilization at the time of this writing exists under the power of women who hold middle management power in business or are given power over the money supplies. And the structure of power continues under women's direct authority inside romantic relationships. Unframed men are held in their feminine frame of authority that they were raised with. There is an ocean of emasculated men under the power of womankind. Man has lost the battle, but we have not lost the war.

By now in the book, and if you have applied my advice into your life, you will notice how women bend to your will when you bear frame. This masculine frame is what calms them under our control. When a man carries frame and has authority in his relationship, his woman will do as he pleases. *She will vote as he pleases.* She will vote against feminism for the health of society. A woman doesn't want the responsibility of destroying civilization. She wants a man to save civilization from her hands. She wants a man to *bear the responsibility of all things.* The feminist experiment is finished. They worship mindless equality above rationality. They use "equity" to justify theft. And nothing is more foolish than replacing hard won competence with emotional inclusion in power positions. Giving power away for shallow arbitrary reasons such as gender and color of skin is supreme corruption. When a competence structure is replaced with crony bricks it will tumble and crumble. *Irrational inclusion will cause the collapse of a society.* The weight of the idiocy shoved to the top of the tower of civilization will cause it to lean and fall under the stress of sheer incompetence. Society is on the brink of failure and it is time to take authority away from womankind.

The madness must end. Men must stand up and assume control before more damage is done. This removal of feminine authority must be done through peace and with their consent. Just as men willingly and peacefully consented to giving away their power to women for "enlightenment" purposes, women will disempower themselves for the greater good. A young generation of men groomed for future leadership will give dignity to us all. We must stop the feminine chaos from destroying all civilization. And it starts with each individual man.

Feminism has encouraged promiscuity which has increased womankind's psychological damage from heartbreak collection. It has destroyed their ability to pair bond which has led them to a solitary existence as men protect themselves from these promiscuous women who cannot even trust themselves, as they have led a life of sexual impulse from following their hearts. As these women age, they become embittered by life by their own sexual decisioning which only fueled their mental illnesses. Their lack of sexual forethought of the future is feminine in design as women lack the capacity for retirement plans since they have relied on men for provisioning for millennia. This will lead to a generation of desperate aging women who will throw away their individual liberties so that they can be saved by an authoritarian government. Feminism has poisoned woman's minds into replacing God with Gov. Their ancestral need for a higher power has twisted their ancestor's religious redemption to state worship without redemption. They worship themselves and their mental illness while dehumanizing mankind as overpopulated. They not only replaced God but also replaced the religious end story with an end story of climate crisis. The framework of religion still exists within them but has been swapped with the thoughts of a few globalist elites. They will stop at nothing until their hive mind spreads throughout the world and assimilates every individual still holding his balls.

"But Jerr," a voice calls out from outside the page, "We will never be able to change our feminist establishment."

Through picking up, carrying and passing frame we will without a doubt change the whole power structure in our ailing civilization. *We will*

reverse a hundred years of feminism. We will
carry frame and pass it to our brother because we
have no other choice. To shrug frame and
complain about women is weak and solves
nothing. That is what our weak forbearers have
been doing while women gain more and more
power over mankind. This emasculation must
stop, and it must stop through peace. We do not
want violence against feminists. We want a
peaceful transition of power through masculine
frame. A woman will support mankind when she
has a brave man leading her way. She will
support her leader for the betterment of the
world. That is how we change our current reality.
*And each man must take passing frame seriously
by passing this book forward.* The feminist
establishment has separated boys from fathers to
further instill in them self-loathing over their
gender and hatred for masculinity. We must
convert a young generation of boys with self-
belief. We must reawaken masculinity like a
lion's roar in the face of our unprecedented
emasculation. We must pass frame because boys
have been orphaned in our forgotten generation.
We must help men *shatter the feminine frame of
authority in their minds* and help free them from
the emotionally weak state they were given from
childhood. It is up to every man to explain his
masculine journey to other men and to share this
book with them. A woman will always feel victim
even when she is lord. For example, feminists in
our time fight for more power while they reign
over mankind. The oppressed mindset never
goes away from a woman no matter how much
power she holds.

Do not selfishly benefit from this book
while men suffer around you. We must help
mankind to rise from its knees. We must fight
against expected censorship and opposition. We

must share word before masculinity is outlawed in every country.

The

wall

crushes

despair

We are born into the light and just as quickly thrown into the dark. Each man cannot kick off the darkness that will someday envelope him. None can escape the black liquid void that will surround us all and rob us of hope. Whether it is heartbreak, violence or a cataclysm of trauma of another sort, we will soon find ourselves in a hopeless and dire state. This hopeless state is like swimming through night while waiting on a dawn that never comes. We feel it a certainty that the sun has forsaken us, and we will be left in the dark for eternity; The hope of any light has left our spirit as we sink down into the abyss of our soul and wish for our own non-existence. This feeling has captured each man and if it has not, it eventually will before he breathes his last breath. This is our human condition; we are all brothers in the darkness of our shared suffering. We are all on the waters of chaos and must swim to the final shore of death. What is a man to do when he feels the sun itself has forsaken him? *He must create his own light.* He must spark the flint of hope within his mind with his own positive actions. He must muster all means at his disposal to resuscitate his own spirit. If a man sees someone drowning, wouldn't he attempt to save them, although a stranger? Should not a man love himself more than a stranger? We must pick ourselves up with the invisible hand of belief that saves us from the darkness of doubt. At the time of writing this I have exhausted my own spirit in this outpouring. My soul aches for a drink of the poison that would make me forget myself. My soul aches for the soft non-existence of liquid pleasure. But I turn away from the siren song of my own destruction because I want to believe in myself. I want to believe in myself, so I can believe in mankind. Because if each man beams like a beacon of hope, then we can all lead each other to shore. I write this book because too many fatherless men have been abandoned to the madness of their existence. They lack meaning in the feminine chaos of their childhoods. My hope for each man is for this book to be the breath needed to revive him back from the floods that have overwhelmed him. We must all join in belief and reassure each other that our lives have more meaning than to simply endure and spread trauma. Create a fire in the dark and invite other men to warm themselves in the night. Life will indeed get darker with each day as we age, but if we create our own light then we will have nothing to fear but our own surrender. Believe in redemption. Even if you raped and pillaged a thousand villages in your life, do not dare surrender to substances that will float you to the end. And do not dare take your life before giving back to mankind what you have robbed. If you surrender from guilty conscience, then your life will only have stolen from the world and your legacy will only exist like a worthless stain. Use the final chapters of your life for the greater good of us all before your last breath pours out and you are taken from this mortal coil. Surrender to the warm embrace of charity and live for your own redemption. And what bigger charity is there in the world than passing masculine frame to men who are stumbling hurt and lost? This external belief in helping others will sink down into the core of your being and will allow peace to grow within.

Many men search out masculine help because their heart has been broken. The "angel" in their mind had lowered herself to earth and went off with another man. From that point on a woman exists perpetually in a state of unknown fidelity. This can tear at a man's spirit if he lets it. But that is what is required to grow up and be a man. To understand the harsh reality of existence and give it a brave face. We cannot control what is outside us, but we can control ourselves and our mind. We can alter our behaviors by picking up frame in order to decrease some chaos. The most important state of mind to have, is to understand that we will never be able to remove chaos completely from our lives. Men get fired from their jobs, get cheated on and eventually die. Floods will come and wipe away our plans without notice.

That is life.

Sometimes a man has despair because his behaviors have reached a point of such weakness that he projects his self-hatred on everyone he sees. This perception will fill his heart with despair only because he despairs in himself, just as the thief who fears thievery.

Or maybe a man surrounds himself with weak friends who lack moral character and only show disbelief in themselves. This can drag a man down from the mire of his societal expectations. If he hangs around these disbelievers-of-self long enough, they will infect his view of reality. His vision will become dark

281

because that is what is being encouraged from those that he surrounds himself with, like a wall of negativity that blocks the rays of positivity from touching his spirit.

There is nothing more beautiful than when a man understands the level of control he has over his body and mind. Along with that, he can control his associates. This control lifts his feet from the swamp of disbelief within himself to the valley of self-belief.

Many men exist in a state of hopelessness because they *feel* alone. There is not a more silly, ignorant and arrogant thought than "aloneness." The world is full of people just like you in large measure. *A man is only alone because he believes himself to be.* To believe in the commonness of self is a blessing to a cursed conscience.

Each man is an iteration of his forebearers and maybe he can add a small measure to their legacy. He is but one page that flips from front to back in his ancestral lineage. There is nothing more arrogant than a man thinking he is alone and original. We are not originals; we are carbon copies of previous things. Do you despair because of sexual abuse? Get in line. Did you abuse another person? Get in line. Are you addicted to alcohol, drugs and pornography? Get in line. Did you have a shit upbringing with abusive parents? Get in line. Plagued with disturbing thoughts? Get in line. Did your woman cheat on you and break your heart? Get in line. Are you unemployed? Get it line. Are you sick and impaired? Get in line. We all suffer together and hopefully we can get to the next day together too.

A man can mold himself into what he wants without letting his past mold him. Don't like yourself? Destroy the old you and be reborn. Do not take your own life, do not give up on your physical body and mind. Be reborn into whatever version of you that helps you to succeed. Become a super organism that adapts to whatever challenging environment that surrounds you. The self can be altered to your own specifications. Weak men allow their crummy upbringing to define them until their last breath. What a waste of human potential that is.

Do not blame the past but rather accept it for what it is. It is merely a beginning for tomorrow. When I say that I believe in you, it comes from my own self-belief. And if I can overcome my life, then why can't you? *Change a history of abuse into a future of belief.* Let us both swim to shore together.

We hope for tomorrow and we can still summon hope for our broken selves to be mended. There is nothing more healing to the spirit than to give a second chance to someone and to be given a second chance. We were all born stumbling confused because of lack of guidance and direction. We were neglected, abused and abandoned but it doesn't define us. *A man must accept full responsibility over himself.* I am not a shaped by my upbringing, it is merely a footnote to my psychology as it should be with yours.

A single mother like all mothers who are dominant will rob a young boy of his belief in self. She doesn't think that is what she's doing but she does it when she protects and coddles him from her own fear of reality. When a mother instills in a boy that she will always be there to mend his wounds is a lie that further traumatizes a boy when he must deal with tragedy without her. A father makes a boy rise alone from a fall not because he is cruel but because he wants the boy to believe in his own capacity for independence. The rise of fatherless men is simultaneous with the rise of disbelievers-of-self. These men exist under the feminine frame of authority because it is a comfort to their lack of self-belief. A man pulls himself up alone not because he is arrogant of help but because he cannot surrender to the void of helplessness within his spirit. Pull yourself up by the bootstraps and afterwards encourage your brother in mankind to do the same.

Despair builds when a man proves to himself with his own weak behaviors (external) that he lacks self-belief (internal). Start proving to yourself that you care with disciplined, healthy habits and let your mind play catch up. Care for yourself and cherish your own existence.

Epilogue

I am a reclusive writer who wrote this book because we have an epidemic of fatherlessness in our times. The mainstream publishers and distributors would not print and market this book. We must become a grassroots movement to get this message out to help others who are struggling. I have learned to take care of myself and have been a one-man-army my whole life. But this time I need help. Please help me to get this message out. *If each man who reads this book is moved enough to share it with the next man, we can change our culture together.* We do not need the establishment to change the world. The Wall Speaks can spread out and help this generation of men. Join us in this masculinity reawakening by recommending this book to others.

Expect that there will be censorship. Expect that there will be smear campaigns and expect all different kinds of persecution. When General Motors was threatened by a book by Ralph Nader, they sent private detectives to dig up dirt on him for character assassination. When MLK was making progress for civil change, the FBI bugged his home and gathered evidence about his extramarital affairs to smear him. And sent him letters urging him to kill himself. *When those in power fear change, they will act recklessly to defend their position.* Emotional and reactionary beings are tyrants. The last half of the twentieth century has seen a massive increase in feminism without censorship. But with the forgotten generation of men reawakening to masculinity, we will without a doubt see censorship and violence at the power transfer. Radical feminists are controlled by emotion and they will not let men rise without persecution. Do not surrender to fear but grow strong in bravery against their feminist tyranny. We must empower men before every society disintegrates from its feminization into the rot of its own chaos. We must empower men before the tower of civilization comes tumbling down from lack of masculine order. It is up to every man to become emboldened in his masculine mission to not only empower himself but to empower his fellow man. We must reawaken masculinity before it becomes outlawed and the tradition becomes extinct. We must awaken the forgotten generation who have been left behind. If the feminist establishment strips me of the right to sell this book, then it is up to you to propagate the message. The message must continue even if the original messenger does not. We all are a messenger of frame and a lifter of mankind. Keep the fire alive within you by passing the torch along and help us conquer our shared global emasculation.

PICK UP,

CARRY AND

PASS FRAME

Made in United States
North Haven, CT
24 August 2023

40709067R00161